SHAHEED AKALI BA

ISBN 978-1-7397401-1-5
KhalisHouse Publishing

www.KhalisHouse.com
info@KhalisHouse.com

Find us on:
Instagram/KhalisHouse
Twitter/KhalisHouse

Khalis House

RANVEER SINGH

For the Khalsa.

RANVEER SINGH

SHAHEED AKALI

BABA DEEP SINGH

RANVEER SINGH

1.

Each droplet was forging its own route down as Nihaal sat by the window, watching the rain race down the glass pane. He observed as some of the droplets collided with others to create a larger ripple before speeding down to the windowsill, where small puddles had gathered. There was the sound of feint background chatter as the Panjabi class murmured in response to the teacher. Nihaal was not paying attention to the class. He was still thinking about *that* meeting.

"Nihaal Singh!" called out Miss Kaur.

Nihaal turned his head towards the front of the class. He felt his classmates' gaze hit his face, which began to turn red.

"Did you hear me?" the teacher asked again.

Nihaal looked around at the familiar faces who seemed to reflect the disappointment beaming down from Miss Kaur.

"*Hanji*, yes, Miss …" Nihaal hesitantly replied.

"So, what is it?"

"I … I was just …" Nihaal stuttered.

"It's *aunkar*!" Nihaal heard Jeet's whisper from behind.

Without thinking, Nihaal shouted, "*aunkar*!"

Miss Kaur didn't hear Jeet whisper the answer to Nihaal. She lowered her hand and turned back towards the class to continue the lesson on *aunkar*, the vowel for 'u' in the Gurmukhi script.

Nihaal turned around and smiled at Jeet before whispering, "Thanks." Jeet nodded and smiled.

Nihaal and Jeet had become friends since joining the Panjabi class five months ago. They only spent a couple of hours together once a week but had already formed a strong bond of friendship. They would sit together in class and the *langar* hall, discussing what each one had been up to during the week.

Nihaal's other siblings were in different classes, and Jeet was an only child, so she really enjoyed spending time with Nihaal. The two were inseparable at the Gurdwara.

Nihaal turned his attention back to the window. The rain had stopped, and the sun had made an appearance.

"Are you still thinking about *the* meeting?" whispered Jeet.

"Yeah, I can't get it out of my head," replied Nihaal.

"Same here; let's go and find Bibi Rano ji after class finishes," Jeet said with excitement.

As the rays of sunlight hit the glass pane, Nihaal closed his eyes momentarily and soaked in the heat. He pictured the scene that Bibi Rano had narrated to him and Jeet last week.

Baba Deep Singh, Banda Singh Bahadur, Baaj Singh, Binod Singh – the names of those at the meeting that Bibi Rano had mentioned ran through Nihaal's mind. Even though she had explained who they were, she had not told them why the Sikh generals had met and what had happened after the meeting. As an inquisitive child, Nihaal naturally had so many questions.

Every time Nihaal heard their names, he felt a deep sense of belonging, like he knew them personally. When Bibi Rano narrated episodes from Sikh history, Nihaal could hear trotting hooves in his head, the gush of water from the rivers of Panjab, and the clash of steel on the battleground. He had heard loads of stories from visiting the Gurdwara, but Bibi Rano had a unique way of storytelling. Every time he heard her speak, it was as if she transported him there, and the entire scene was playing out in front of his eyes. He could see the action, feel the emotion, and hear the war cries through Bibi Rano's voice.

Miss Kaur finished the class and the children began packing their bags. Jeet hurriedly put her books away, flung her backpack on to her shoulder, and then helped Nihaal with his bag. They waited for the other children to leave before Jeet held the door open. They headed down the corridor to the main foyer and then towards the lift.

Some of the children from the other classes ran past them towards the stairs.

"I hope there's *kheer* today," said Nihaal as they waited for the lift to come down.

"Mmm … *kheer*!" replied Jeet. The thought of sweet rice pudding made her mouth water. The lift arrived, and they walked in.

"I was thinking *that* meeting must have been really important because it brought together such great Sikh leaders," Nihaal said.

"Yeah, it was almost as if Bibi Rano was reeling off the name of every Sikh whose painting hangs around the *langar* hall!"

Nihaal nodded in agreement.

The lift doors opened, and the two friends walked out to the sound of clanging steel plates and cups that resonated from the open *langar* hall doors. Kirtan could also be heard blaring out of the speakers on the wall. They headed for the *langar* hall and peered inside.

"I don't see her," said Nihaal

"She's probably in the kitchen area with the other Bibia," Jeet replied.

"Come on then, let's go!" Nihaal said.

"No, wait, we have to go and take our shoes off first, Nihaal!" said Jeet.

The two friends headed off towards the cloakrooms. They took off their shoes, washed their hands, and then walked back to the *langar* hall. It was busy inside, as it usually was on a Sunday after the Panjabi classes finished. Some children were sat in *pangat* rows on the floor, eating *langar*, others were in the queue, and some were running around. Nihaal and Jeet joined the queue, moving as slowly as ever.

"I still don't see her," said Nihaal as he peered into the open kitchen behind the *sevadars* serving *langar*.

"Look, there she is," said Jeet.

Without thinking, Nihaal shouted, "Bibi Rano ji!"

"Shhhh, you can't shout in here, Nihaal," said Jeet.

"Why not? It's not exactly quiet, is it?" he replied.

One of the *sevadars* frowned at Nihaal, but he was too busy smiling and waving at Bibi Rano to notice.

Bibi Rano was cutting lettuce when she heard the all too familiar voice of Nihaal. She looked up and saw him standing in the *langar* queue beside Jeet grinning from cheek to cheek and waving frantically. She smiled and waved back.

As they neared the front, Nihaal moved his *taal* forward for the *sevadars* who served hot *daal, kheer,* and a *parshada.* Jeet followed as they both filled their *taals* with warm and delicious *langar* before taking a seat on the floor with the rest of the *Sangat.*

"*D-dha data ek hai ...*" Jeet began to sing the Shabad a Sikh recites before eating. Nihaal joined in "*... sabh ko*

7

devanhaar." They recited the entire Shabad and then quickly ate their *langar.*

After taking their *taals* to the area where the *sevadars* were cleaning, Nihaal and Jeet headed to the corner where Bibi Rano had sat down with a cup of *cha.*

"Ajo mere puth." Bibi Rano pushed her glasses down her nose and welcomed the two children as if they were her own. This was how she was, always very welcoming to all.

"Bibi Rano ji, can you tell us more about that meeting between Baba Deep Singh and Banda Singh Bahadur?" Nihaal didn't waste any time.

"Well, *puth*, that meeting was always going to happen because of what the Guru had initiated," said Bibi Rano before taking a sip of her *cha.*

"What did the Guru initiate?" asked Nihaal.

"Okay, if you want to know more about that meeting, and learn about what the Guru had initiated, take a seat here." Bibi Rano motioned the children to sit down and adjusted her *chunni.*

Nihaal and Jeet sat on the floor. Bibi Rano took another sip of her *cha.* The noise in the *langar* hall seemed to quieten as she began the story.

"The year was 1755 ..."

2.

"Save us!" "Save us!" Baba ji! "Please save us!"

"We have been beaten; they have looted us … they have taken everything … please save us!"

Covered in blood, a man and woman stumbled forward. They were badly beaten and bruised all over. The man's clothes were ripped, and the woman's clothes were partially missing. The man was trying to cover her by keeping her close to him. As they neared the *divan*, the woman lost her balance. She fell to the ground, pulling the man down with her.

A couple of Singhs from the *divan* immediately leapt forward to help the couple. One Singh took off his *hazoori* and flung it around the woman's torso. The other called out for medical attention. Within seconds, another Singh arrived with water, towels, and bandages.

Hearing the commotion outside, Baba Deep Singh quickly placed a *rumala sahib* over Maharaj. He signalled the others to take over and then jumped up to head outside. Baba Deep Singh moved towards the crowd that had

9

gathered and then turned to the man and asked, "It is okay; you are in a safe space now. Tell me, who did this to you? Who beat you? Who looted you?"

Wiping his face with a towel, the man looked up and said, "Baba ji, we were travelling to a village called Satae."

The blood from his forehead continued to pour down as he desperately wiped it away before one of the Singhs laid him down and applied some compression on the wound.

"What is your name, son?" asked Baba Deep Singh.

"My name is Karam Chand … I was walking with my teenage daughter, son, and his wife to their village …"

Gesturing to the woman, he continued, "This is my wife … she was with me. On the way, some of Bhatti Nasir Din's men stopped us. They started to harass us and asked for money. We did not have anything of value on us. My son tried to intervene, but they began to beat him."

Pausing for a moment, Karam Chand looked over to his wife before continuing, "They killed our son! Then they beat me and my wife until we fell unconscious. When we regained consciousness, they were gone, as were the few possessions we had on us. They kidnapped my daughter and daughter-in-law."

Baba Deep Singh asked, "Where did they attack you?"

"About three miles from here … they were on horseback. They must have rode off back towards the north," replied Karam Chand.

"Partap Singh! Ready the horses … we are to leave right away," said Baba Deep Singh.

He turned back towards Karam Chand to reassure him. "You are safe here. The Singhs will take care of you.

The Singhs were *parupkari,* which meant they always looked out for the welfare of others. This is key teaching within the Sikh way of life. They could not bear to see others in pain. Just hearing of their ordeal made them forget any personal unease of hunger or thirst. The Singhs were famous for selflessly serving others and saving them from the clutches of ego-fuelled men that occupied positions of power and control in the region.

All residents of the Lakhi Jungle near Tabo Ki Talwandi, where they resided, knew of the Singhs and held great respect for them. The area's residents looked towards the Singhs for protection and shelter.

"Singhs cannot ignore the cries of help from the weak and innocent. Fighting and dying for *dharam,* the righteous cause, and protecting the oppressed is what we have learned. It is our duty to take on this service for the Panth," said one of the Singhs.

Within a few moments, one hundred Singhs on horseback emerged from the grounds of the *divan.* Karam Chand sat up, placing his hand above his eyes to catch a glimpse of their swords, which glistened like lightning bolts. Their spears in hand were like hissing tongues of snakes ready to pounce at any given moment, and the *chakars* upon their *dumallay* lit up the sky. Sitting atop Iranian horses, the finest breeds reserved for kings, adorned in blue and yellow, the *jatha* of Singhs marched along the narrow path, led by Baba Deep Singh, whose eyes were full of *bir-ras*. There was a huge cloud of dust as the horses cried out, leapt forward, and galloped out of Sabo Ki Talwandi.

Bhatti Nasir Din was a local leader infamously known for terrorising the locals and taking their loot. He had occupied thirty villages and readily taxed the residents or threatened them with violence. He had camped up in Fort Peera, approximately eight miles southeast of Sabo Ki Talwandi, Damdama Sahib. It no longer stands today because the Singhs later reduced the fort's walls to sand dunes.

As brave and daring as Baba Deep Singh was, he was equally compassionate and caring. His *dharmic* qualities were known to all; he was a saintly warrior. Whether sitting or standing, he would often be seen reciting Gurbani. Every act in service of the Panth was completed with the recital of a Shabad, which reverberated Baba Deep Singh's whole being. He greeted everyone with love and respect but was a force to be reckoned with for anyone who dared to exploit the vulnerable and abuse their position of power.

The area surrounding Fort Peera included poor Muslims and Hindus. Keeping them in mind, Baba Deep Singh proclaimed, "We will stop some distance from the fort and send a message to Nasir Din to come and meet us outside. He will bring the two innocent women out, or else swords will be swung, and he will feel the wrath of the Guru's Singhs."

As the Singhs neared the fort, some of Nasir Din's men stationed in the watch towers immediately sent a message for the fort gates to be closed. They also informed Nasir Din of the Singhs' arrival. When the message reached him, he was struck with a sudden sense of fear; he knew why the Singhs had arrived, and his fear quickly turned to panic.

As it happened, on this occasion, Nasir Din was not responsible for kidnapping the women or beating and killing Karam Chand's son. He had been in the fort all morning; however, he was aware of some commotion in the courtyard that morning. As he looked around, a messenger appeared with a note outlining Baba Deep Singh's ultimatum. Fearing for his life, Nasir Din immediately picked up a white flag and asked the guards to open the Fort gates. He walked out with a couple of attendants, crossed the path, and headed towards Baba Deep Singh and the *jatha* of Singhs.

As he neared them, he mercifully raised his hand and cried out, "Baba ji, in the name of Allah, I had no hand in what happened. Some of my men arrived earlier with the women; I did not tell them to do what they did."

He came forward and stopped in front of Baba Deep Singh before placing the white flag at his feet. Clasping his hands, he continued, "Please forgive them. Please come with me into the fort. I am your servant."

Baba Deep Singh looked at Nasir Din before replying, "The two Hindu women in your possession. Where are they, and who brought them here?!"

Hearing the roar of the lion, Nasir Din started to tremble.

Baba Deep Singh was in no mood to hear Nasir Din's excuses. He had travelled to confront and deliver justice to Nasir Din for his men's actions. He was angry because Nasir Din was a Panjabi; he was of the land, yet under his watch. His men had attacked their own people and kidnapped women for their own pleasure. It was one thing when foreign invaders arrived to plunder, loot, and kidnap, but it was another when individuals like Nasir Din condoned this type of action upon his own people.

With sweat dripping down his face, Nasir Din pulled at his collar before replying, "Maharaj! Two women have certainly been brought here, but I did not take them, nor did I know of this happening until they were brought here. I have already punished the men for their actions. Please come down off your horse and follow me. I will present them before you."

Baba Deep Singh was a fearless warrior; he turned and scoped the vicinity before dismounting his horse. Accompanied by five other Singhs, who were fully armed, he headed towards the fort. They entered the *divan khana*, where Nasir Din's eldest *begum* brought both women to the room.

Addressing Baba Deep Singh, the *begum* spoke.

"Pita ji!" she exclaimed with clasped hands, "these women have been kept here with the utmost respect; my husband is not at fault for any wrongdoing."

This *begum* had already saved Nasir Din's life before. She had pleaded with Baba Deep Singh to spare his life following a previous clash. At that time, she had dropped to her knees and asked Baba Deep Singh to take her as his own daughter and save her the burden of becoming a widow. At that point, the merciful Baba Deep Singh had accepted her plea, and from that point onwards, she always referred to him as her father.

"Child …" spoke Baba Deep Singh, "one who commits the wrong action must be held to account. We came here to smash this fort to pieces, but …"

In those days, Singhs were of high moral character and lived truthfully. Hindu and Muslim women did not fear the Singhs, nor did they ever feel in danger. On the contrary, they would often be relieved when in their presence. They had belief in the Singhs, who viewed and respected other women the same as their own mothers, daughters, and sisters.

"Please ask these two young women. We have treated them like our own daughters. They have shared their pain with me, and it is regrettable that one lost her husband and the other her brother. We have already captured the culprits for you," spoke the *begum.*

She thanked Baba Deep Singh for riding out with the Singhs and expressed her gratitude for listening to her. As Baba Deep Singh turned towards Nasir Din, the *begum* spoke again, "We heard news of Ahmad Shah Durrani's raid on Delhi ... he stopped off in Mathra, Bindraban, Agra, Aligarh and other places where he ransacked the towns and took a lot of loot."

Baba Deep Singh turned back towards the *begum,* who continued, "We have also heard that he has kidnapped thousands of women he will take back to Afghanistan. Even if all the Hindus and Muslims united, they could not stop him."

The *begum* continued to narrate the events of Ahmad Shah Durrani's invasion as she had heard them. Nasir Din stood in silence, not moving an inch. Some time passed in conversation before Nasir Din offered a thousand rupees to Baba Deep Singh and the Singhs, which they duly accepted. They returned to their horses with the two women who had been taken. The culprits responsible for the vicious attack and murder of Karam Chand's son were tied to the back of the horses.

The Singhs pulled back the reins to direct the horses towards Damdama Sahib. Upon arriving back in Sabo Ki Talwandi, the women were returned to their family, who the medics had treated in the Singhs' *jatha*. The two culprits had succumbed to their injuries, but their corpses were shown to Karam Chand, who clasped his hands in gratitude towards the Singhs. He mourned the loss of his son but thanked the Singhs for returning his daughters to safety.

Evening arrived, and the sun began to set. Baba Deep Singh swiftly bathed and got ready to join the *Sangat* for *Rehras Sahib.* This was followed by *Bhog* and *Ardas,* after which Baba Deep Singh turned to talk with an elder Singh. However, just as he was about to speak, there was some commotion outside. Seconds later, the sound of a *nagara* could be heard, and a representative of the Dal Khalsa entered the *divan* and read a *hukamnama:*

"This Order from the Jathedar of the Dal Khalsa summons you to join them. Durrani has looted Delhi and is on his way back to Afghanistan. You are to make your way towards the Emperor's Road and await further instructions."

Baba Deep Singh asked, "Where is Durrani at this moment?"

"He has left Delhi but has not yet reached Thanesar. We are to strike from the banks of the Satluj," came the response.

Baba Deep Singh nodded and spoke, "We accept this *hukam* from the Dal Khalsa and consider ourselves fortunate to answer the call and, if need be, give our heads in service of the Panth." Then turning to the Jatha of

Singhs, he invoked the Guru's words, "We know only the way of the Guru – *jau tau prem khelan ka chao sir tar tali gali meri aao.*"

With that, Baba Deep Singh gave instructions for the Singhs to prepare the horses and battle standards.

*****

"Who is the Dal Khalsa," asked Nihaal. He hadn't budged since Bibi Rano had begun the story.

"The Dal Khalsa, son, was formed by Nawab Kapur Singh in 1734. It was an army comprised of the Budha Dal and Taruna Dal. Their role was to further the Panth's objectives and fight oppression. At the time of this story, however, the Jathedar of the Dal Khalsa was Sardar Jassa Singh Ahluwalia."

Nihaal looked up at the images on the walls of the *langar* hall before he found the famous image of Sardar Jassa Singh Ahluwalia on horseback.

"Bibi Rano ji, when was Baba Deep Singh ji born, and what was he like as a child?" asked Jeet.

Bibi Rano smiled and then softly said, "I'll tell you, as I have heard it from my elders."

3.

Baba Deep Singh was a complete Gursikh of Guru Gobind Singh ji. His bravery and leadership qualities were known to all residents of Lakhi Jungle. He was also a great scholar who dedicated time to spreading Gurmat. He was born in the famous village of Pahuvind, in the Majha region of Panjab. His father's name was Bhai Bhagtu, and his mother's name was Bibi Jeeuni.

Bhai Bhagtu lived up to his name. He would spend many hours meditating and serve travelling Sadhus and Gursikhs with full devotion. Everyone enjoyed spending time with Bhai Bhagtu; he was lovingly known as Bhagat ji.

Bibi Jeeuni also lived up to her name. From a young age, she was wise and carried herself with grace. Her entire being radiated with love, which everyone who met her felt. She would work hard in the house's upkeep and accompany her husband to work the fields. Bibi Jeeuni would also cycle to Sri Anandpur Sahib to have the *darshan* of Guru Gobind Singh. Both husband and wife had open fields with good crops and cattle; fellow villagers respected them well, but inside they were a little sad. Behind their smiles was sadness because they did not have a child.

Both Bhai Bhagtu and Bibi Jeeuni were healthy and fit. Their bodies did not suffer from any physical ailment, nor did they have any other medical conditions preventing them from having children. They were both of age and ready to have children, but only the True Creator knew why no child had been born in their house. The entire universe works according to the *hukam* of *Akal Purakh*; the entire world play is conducted under that *hukam*.

The year was 1682, the month of Magh had passed, and the season of Basant was upon them. Bhai Bhagtu and Bibi Jeeuni were in their fields, sitting on top of a small cabin that housed some cattle. They had just finished repairing the well system and were awaiting the arrival of some other workers to complete the task of refitting the large wheel. Both husband and wife were sat talking. Beside them was a basket of millet *rotis*, with some fruit, sugar canes, and cool refreshing *lassis*.

As they were talking, Bhai Bhagtu noticed a stranger walking towards their field. The man was wearing a colourful *chola* and his face radiated a divine light. He had a white beard, and as he neared them, he called out,

"Beloved Sikhs of the Guru, Sat Kartar!"

"Sat Kartar!", both husband and wife replied with folded hands and climbed down from the small cabin.

Out of respect, Bhai Bhagtu went to touch the elderly Gursikh's feet, but he stopped him and clasped his hands around Bhai Bhagtu's folded hands before pulling him in for a loving embrace.

"Beloveds of Guru, *dhan ho tusi,*" you are great said the elderly man.

As he sat down beside them, Bibi Jeeuni offered the elderly man some food and water, which he duly accepted with folded hands. Bhai Bhagtu jumped up to grab some water before pouring it for the elderly man to wash his hands. Bibi Jeeuni served the millet *roti,* adding fresh butter and a portion of yoghurt. The elderly man thanked them and began to eat. Bhai Bhagtu felt a deep sense of love and rejoiced at having served the travelling man who appeared to him in the image of *Bhai Dhanna,* the 15th-century poet. Some of his writings were added to the Guru Granth Sahib by Guru Arjan Sahib.

Bibi Jeeuni's character was such that whenever she served someone, whether food and water or offered clothes and shelter to travelling Sadhus, she felt great joy whenever she served someone. She saw all that she had as a gift from the Guru, so to be able to share that with others made her happy. She was not proud or driven by a sense of ego to serve, but she did so out of her own kind heart and love for the Creator and Creation. She was illiterate but knew many of the Guru's Shabads, and one came to her at that moment – *sabh meh varte eko soe gur parsadi pargat hoe.*

21

She thought to herself, *everything we have is a gift from Akal Purakh; a person only works hard to serve what is bestowed by Akal Purakh. They live their lives in this service.* She had heard many such nuggets of wisdom while sitting in Sangat and listening to Gurbani, that Akal Purakh is the provider and sustainer of life.

As these thoughts ran through her mind, Bibi Jeeuni began visualizing how Baba Buddah ji and Mata Ganga ji had also longed for a child. She thought, *I have longed to have a child play in my lap for fifteen years. Only a Sikh of Sache Patshah can bless me with such a gift.*

At that moment, the elderly man recognised Bibi Jeeuni's internal desire of motherhood. Without her uttering a word, he understood how she longed for a child. He looked up at them both, smiled, and then continued to eat. Then he spoke, "Bibi ji, the *lassi* is very sweet."

"Satguru has blessed us with cattle; they are the ones who produce this sweet milk that I have served you," replied Bibi Jeeuni.

"The millet *roti* is Amrit-like; they have been prepared with love and faith."

"Just as the Creator has provided the grains, so too has the Creator arranged this meal for Sikhs to prepare. I have just served this; all praise goes to the Creator," replied Bibi Jeeuni.

The elderly Sikh ate the *roti* before Bibi Jeeuni served him some more. As she placed the *roti* into his hands, the

Sikh looked around the place. Noticing no children were running around, he smiled and spoke, "Beloved Sikhs of the Guru, you have a great piece of land here; you are very fortunate. You have a sustainable life where you grow your own food and raise your own cattle."

"Gurmukho, this is all provided for by Akal Purakh. We are just servants here, as the Creator orders. We work hard, but all this is because of the Creator's grace. This well, the field, the crops, the cattle, our tools and means of living, all of it is due to the blessings of Vaheguru," said Bhai Bhagtu.

The elderly man nodded and smiled again. His face continued to radiate with a heavenly glow, and his eyes glistened. Turning around, he spoke, "I don't see any children here."

Hearing these words, Bibi Jeeuni lowered her eyes, and her heart skipped a beat.

"We are all Sikhs of the Great Guru; what worth is there in keeping anything from you …" said Bhai Bhagtu.

"We do not have any children but accept this is the *hukam* of Akal Purakh. Perhaps we are guilty of some crime that has kept us from receiving the blessings of a child, but only the Creator knows. We yearn for a child, to play in our laps, to run through these fields and one day work with us on our land, but we also accept that maybe it is not in our destiny to have a child."

Bibi Jeeuni had been married to Bhai Bhagtu for fifteen years; she was ready for a child and longed for motherhood. Listening to her husband speak, Bibi Jeeuni's eyes teared up. Like pearls, they slowly rolled down before resting on her cheeks. The tears conveyed her heart's desire to bear a child and enter motherhood.

The elderly Sikh saw the tears. He then uttered the wisdom of Bhairao Mahala 5 – *"cheeti aave ta maha anand, cheet aave ta sabhi dukh bhanj."*

He completed the Shabad and addressed the couple again.

"You are both Sikhs of the Guru; you sing the praises of Akal Purakh, you accept and live in *hukam*, and your wish for a child will be granted one day. A great warrior, a saint-soldier, will arrive in this house. This is all in the play of Akal Purakh. You must continue to keep the faith and stay close to the Guru's House."

Bibi Jeeuni felt an instant pang of happiness radiate through her entire being. Tears of happiness now filled her eyes. She felt a great sense of love, as though through the *hukam* of Satguru, Baba Buddha ji had spoken those words himself.

The elderly Sikh finished his food, stood, and recited an Ardas for the *chardikala* of the couple and for Akal Purakh to complete their acceptance of *hukam*.

After a little while, the Sikh clasped his hands and spoke again, "Right, okay, let's do some work … I'll start the roller press; you bring over the sugar canes. Let's make some *gur*."

"Please sit and relax. We will see to the work. It'll be done in no time at all, and then you can enjoy the sweetness of the sugar canes," said Bhai Bhagtu before jumping up and walking towards the sugar cane roller press.

The elderly Sikh jumped up like a young athlete and ran over to the roller press. Bhai Bhagtu laughed, took the signal to collect the sugar canes, and Bibi Jeeuni joined him. The three worked the roller press and began working on the sugar canes.

They worked together for five days. Bibi Jeeuni was very happy; everything within their home began to appear vibrant and colourful. The plants appeared greener, the birds sounded sweeter, the water tasted fresher, and the air was lighter. Just as the elderly Sikh had entered their life out of nowhere, he disappeared in the same way. The couple knew nothing about his address or which village he had come from.

A few months passed, and the Sikh's *ardas* was answered. Bibi Jeeuni shared the news with Bhai Bhagtu they had both been longing for; she was pregnant. Everyone in the village came to congratulate the couple. The summer season passed, and winter soon arrived. On 18th Magh 1739 Bikrami, which fell on 26th January 1682, Bibi Jeeuni gave birth to a beautiful child.

"It's a boy!" said the midwife. Bibi Jeeuni and Bhai Bhagtu named the child Deep.

4.

In those days, the Mughal emperor of Delhi was Aurangzeb. The Hindu Hill Rajas also governed various principalities across the region. Together the Mughals and the Hindu Hill Rajas controlled large areas. While their writ ran far and wide, in Panjab, there was relative peace due to the establishment of the Guru's Darbar. *Sants* and *fakirs* would roam freely, meeting one another for divine discourse, serving and helping society. Due to the wisdom imparted by the Guru, many people broke away from idol worship and renunciation. Many gave up their old ways that had become polluted with empty ritualism. The land of Panjab saw many people walk on the path of the Gurmukhs. Instead of focusing on outwardly dress and physical penances, the Guru had shown the path to *mukhti*, liberation, lay within. The instruction from the Guru was to take the inner journey, which would lead one to find that Akal Purakh resided deep within. There was no need to visit places of pilgrimage and perform various physical penances and austerities. Neither was there the need to wear a particular thread or smear the body with ashes. The

26

divisions and sects that people had created were criticised for creating a hierarchy where the people who occupied positions of authority and control had led society astray. Prior to the Guru's arrival, human consciousness lay shattered in pieces. Disconnected from divine truth, it revolved around the circle of material tendencies. The Guru broke the falsehood that had enraptured the masses by revealing the wisdom of the *shabad*, joining people to *nam,* and exposing the pitfalls of attaching oneself to the material world. By centring the divine and creating *sangat* where the praises of Akal Purakh were sung, the Guru had built a society of the Gurmukhs.

Bhai Bhagtu and Bibi Jeeuni raised their son with love and amongst the Sangat of the Gurmukhs. He was showered with the blessings of a Sikh household and spent his infant years playing within the gardens of his parent's land. Before they knew it, young Deep was five years old, and he began to visit the well, assisted with cutting sugar canes, milking the cows, and collecting wood. Bhai Bhagtu read Gurbani to Deep, and he soon came to learn many *shabads* off by heart. He spent his childhood in this way, playing, working, and reciting Gurbani with his parents. Deep was a favourite amongst the village and would often be seen helping the villagers. He also had a lot of love and affection for wildlife and would spend many hours a day playing in the forests close to his village. His circle of friends would join him, and collectively they would build shelters for animals that were otherwise targets for poachers, hunted for their skin or ivory.

Deep's infant years flew by, and soon enough, young Deep turned eighteen. He had a strong physique from the years spent working on his family farm, but he was a gentle and loving soul. He was one of the tallest in his circle of friends, but he also had the most sweet and melodious voice. He played *sochi* and *kabaddi* with his friends, wrestled, and took an interest in riding horses. He participated in many sports competitions in his village, and news of his athleticism had spread to neighbouring villages across Malwa too. In training and sports, he would often be the leader; everyone respected him.

A year or so earlier, at the Vaisakhi of 1699, Guru Gobind Singh ji had created the Khalsa and revealed the Panj Pyar-e to the whole world. Whoever had attended came away and spread the news across their village. The news spread like wildfire, and many came to know of how five souls from different walks of life had stood up and given their heads to the Guru.

This year many people across Majha were preparing to travel to Anandpur Sahib and receive Amrit so that they could become initiated Khalsa too. Young Deep had heard about the Vaisakhi of 1699 from the villagers too. He came home one day and addressed Bibi Jeeuni,

"Ma, I have heard about the incredible power of the Guru who resides at Anandpur Sahib. A great gathering was called last year, where a large tent was constructed for the revelation of the Khalsa. I heard that the Guru called for five Sikhs to come forward and offer their heads to the Guru. He beheaded all five before fixing each head onto a different torso!"

"Yes, son. That is what happened. Their power and praise are immeasurable," replied Bibi Jeeuni.

Bibi Jeeuni looked at her youthful son, full of life and vigour. She brought him close and hugged him tightly. Then she placed her hand on his head and blessed him.

"Son, the Guru's power and strength are divine and have no limits or boundaries. We cannot understand the ways of the Guru with mere intellect of the mind. We are a sacrifice unto their ways. This has been the way since Guru Nanak Sahib arrived and initiated this path of Gursikhi from Kartarpur Sahib."

"I used to go a lot to have *darshan* of the Guru. Anandpur Sahib is the most magical place. It has been a part of the Guru's House since Guru Tegh Bahadur ji. The Guru's Sahibzade have grown up in the hills of Anandpur Sahib and there is much to learn from those who reside there. It has been a few years now since I last went …"

"Then, we should go too, Ma," Deep interjected, "how far is it?" he asked.

"It is quite far, son, over a hundred miles away."

29

"That doesn't matter … it just means it will take us about four or five days to travel by foot," replied Deep, "we'll travel with the rest of the Sangat and get there together."

Bibi Jeeuni looked at her son and smiled. She spoke again, "Okay, go and get ready. We'll see to the harvest upon our return." She turned and looked towards the field before continuing, "The wheat is still green but should ripen and turn golden brown when we return."

Deep's eyes widened, and his face lit up.

"I'll have to sew up a new *kurta;* we have the sheet of cloth to make it at home," said Bibi Jeeuni.

"But I've heard the Guru has given a specific *hukam,*" said Deep.

"Oh really, what's that?"

"When coming to have *darshan*, all Sikhs, whether old or young, men, women or children, must wear certain items."

"What items must we wear?"

"Well, the order from Anandpur Sahib is that we must not wear a *dhoti* but a *kachera.* In fact, we should have two with us."

"Why is that?"

"To make sure the spare one can be worn after bathing. There is a strict requirement not to wear the *dhoti*. I have also heard that we need to wear a round bracelet made of iron, carry a sword, spear, shield, and bring horses."

"Dhan Guru Nanak," said Bibi Jeeuni.

"You sew the *kachera,* Ma. We have our horse; I'll have a spear made … and the rest of the items we'll get on route or from there. Ma, I have also heard the Guru disallows the cutting of hair …"

"Yes, son. This is why we have not cut your hair for two years now. Our previous actions now remain in the distant past."

"Very well, Ma. Then we must definitely go. Taru, Garja, and Beant are all going too. I'll go and find out what time everyone is leaving. I saw the Guru's messenger speaking to the *sarpanch* earlier."

"Go, son. May the Guru bless you. Be quick, we have to collect some flour, sugar, and *ghee,* to take for the Guru's *langar,* too. I'll make a start on the *kacheras."*

Deep was ecstatic! Just as a young child grasps a new toy from his mother and runs away in joy to play with it, he skipped out of the house, his mind full of exciting thoughts about meeting the Guru for the first time. He felt as though he was about to embark on a journey of a lifetime. He had grown up listening to the stories from his father and elders in the village about how the Sikh Panth was initiated with the founding of Kartarpur Sahib at the beginning of the 16th century. He recalled the line in Sidh Gost where Guru Nanak Sahib explained how the *udassis*, the long journeys Guru Sahib had taken in all four directions, were started with a purpose. The purpose was to find the Gurmukhs.

Gurmukh khojat bhei udassi, ran through Deep's mind.

Some of Bhai Gurdas ji's *vaaran*, which further elaborated on this, also came to mind. The Guru had started the *udassis* in search of the Gurmukhs, but the Gurmukhs were nowhere to be seen. The world was divided, engrossed in falsehood, corruption, greed, and ego.

This is why Guru Nanak Sahib founded Kartarpur Sahib. It was a space to nurture the Gurmukhs through *sangat* and *nam*. Deep had been told from a young age that Sikh sovereignty was integral to the Sikh Panth. It is why the Sikhs referred to the Guru not as a mere teacher or holy man but as Sache Patshah, the true sovereign of both worlds. Each of the Guru Sahiban added to the Panth by founding new towns and cities. The Gurmukhi script was created to instil a new sense of identity for the Gurmukhs. An identity centred on the divine. Where the Guru Sahiban encouraged meditation and *bhagti*, they also encouraged physical training, wrestling, and horse riding.

The Guru Sahiban sat on thrones, created parallel power structures, spread Gurmat, raised armies, and waged war under the sovereign flags of Guru Nanak Sahib. From Kartarpur Sahib came Khadur Sahib, then Goindval Sahib, Tarn Taran Sahib, Amritsar Sahib, Kiratpur Sahib and Anandpur Sahib. Where the Guru bestowed the wisdom of the *shabad* and opened the inner door so people could walk the journey from being *manmukhs* to becoming Gurmukhs, they also laid a path to physical liberation.

The journey that Guru Nanak Sahib initiated in search of the Gurmukhs led to the creation of the Panth, where the agency and authority of the Guru reigned. Deep thought about all this and felt he, too, was about to join that revolution. Little did he know how the call from Anandpur Sahib wouldn't just bring him onto the path of Sikhi but change the course of history for him and Panjab.

5.

The power of faith and love is very great. When these qualities exist within a man and a woman, they can move mountains. The power of love is the power of God.

Beloved Sikhs of the Guru's House would travel hundreds of miles on this power of faith and love to reach Anandpur Sahib. They had *darshan* of Sache Patshah, took part in *seva* and *sangat,* listened to *kirtan,* and took the blessings of listening to the wisdom imparted by the Guru. The land of Anandpur Sahib gave new hope to thousands of travellers who arrived there. Upon entering the Khalsa fold, they would return home full of love and a yearning to walk on the path of the Gurmukhs.

The *sangat* of Majha gathered in the town of Chabaal ten days before the Vaisakhi of 1700. Bhai Bhagtu, Bibi Jeeuni, and their son, Deep, arrived from the village of Pahuvind alongside their neighbours. Their clothes, horses, weapons, and carts of raw ingredients were with them. They set off and soon arrived in Hoshiarpur and then neared the Satluj with the number of *sangat* growing through each town. For

Deep, seeing different *sangat* and walking through so many new towns was an exciting experience. He walked the entire way, leaving his mother and father to take turns and sit atop their horse. Bibi Jeeuni tried very hard to make him sit on the horse, but he respectfully said, "Mother, it's okay. You stay seated. I am fine walking."

He continued, "In fact, I want to walk the whole way to Anandpur Sahib. They say if you walk to the Guru's house, you are blessed with the dust of the *sangat's* feet," implying that walking with the *sangat* brings humility.

Walking with Deep was a family including two sisters, a *bharjai, chachi,* and the *chachi's* two sons. They were happily talking amongst one another; some were singing s*habads* while holding each other's hands. One of the sisters looked up at Bibi Jeeuni and said, "Mata ji, your son is enjoying the walk, and you are enjoying the ride, so why do you insist on walking? Let him walk. You watch; one day, Deep will walk many miles to answer the Guru's call."

Bibi Jeeuni smiled. She looked at Deep, steadfast and determined to walk the whole way. She noticed the spring in his step, anticipating and readying himself to have *darshan* of the Tenth Master at Anandpur Sahib. As that thought crossed her mind, she heard the Satluj, at which moment she turned towards the hills and saw the Nishan Sahibs flying high above the Guru's Darbar. The forts of Anandpur stood as high as the mountains.

"Dhan Dhan Sache Patshah, Dhan DhanKalgidhar Pita, Dhan Dhan Satguru ji!" she said, which many echoed in the *kafla*. They crossed the Satluj and headed towards Anandpur Sahib. Tens of thousands had flocked there to celebrate Vaisakhi. Rows of makeshift tents had been set up as far as the eye could see. Bhai Bhagtu, Bibi Jeeuni, and Deep took a spot along the wall opposite the Guru's Darbar. Everywhere they looked, the Guru's praise was being sung. The town was full of colour, and everything appeared majestic to Deep. He saw Sikh warriors holding various weapons as they walked through the town. Many of the youth felt inspired upon seeing them move with such poise. Deep was completely mesmerised by the Khalsa and the surroundings of Anandpur Sahib.

"Amrit, the nectar prepared within the iron bowl and stirred with the double-edged sword, will be ready soon. Whoever wishes to take Amrit, prepare to present yourselves in the Guru's Darbar. Two *kachere*, a *kirpan*, *kanga* and *kara* is the insignia of a Sikh; you must bring these with you. If you do not have any, then you may come and see one of the *sevadars*, and they will provide these for you." Deep listened to the Sikh warrior address the *sangat*.

Many people went into their tents while others flocked to the *sevadars* to ask for some of the *kakkars*. Deep collected his own *kakkar* and stood waiting with his mother and father.

The Panj Pyar-e prepared the Amrit, and the *sangat* were called into the large *divan* that had been laid out. Kirtan was sung as the *sangat* sat down. Guru Gobind Singh ji arrived and addressed the *sangat,* speaking about the initiation into the Khalsa and the importance of *Rehat Maryada*, the code of conduct. Deep watched and listened as the Guru spoke of creating an army called the Khalsa. Akal Purakh was their support. The army's mission was to protect the weak, uproot tyrants, and create a prosperous society where all could live without fear and hatred. Those who entered the Khalsa army were to accept the name Singh or Kaur. They were not to fear anyone, nor would they frighten anyone. Whosoever attained *shaheedi* would become immortal. He or she would find a place at the feet of Akal Purakh.

On that day, thousands took Amrit, of which Deep was one. He accepted the *hukam* of Satguru and, upon taking Amrit, became Deep Singh.

"Now you have become a Singh," spoke the Guru.

"You must remember the following. These weapons that have now become an extension of your arms must only be used to defend the weak, fight tyranny, and to further the Panth. These weapons must not be used to hurt or frighten the innocent; they are your friends to advance *dharam,* righteousness. Do not betray the Panth with these weapons. Secondly, from this point forward, you are to eulogise Akal Purakh, live the way of the Khalsa, and spread the wisdom of *shabad*. You must keep the *panj kakkar* – *kanga, kachera, kirpan, karra* and *kes*. You must refrain from using tobacco, cutting your hair, eating halal meat, or committing adultery."

Deep Singh listened to the Guru's words while taking in the magnitude of the moment. He felt a strong sense of belonging standing in front of the Guru and amongst the Khalsa in Anandpur Sahib. He listened attentively to the Guru's final instructions about devoting mind, body, and soul to the Panth, and then bowed in acceptance of the *hukam*, completing the pledge of allegiance to the Guru's House. He then sat down in the *divan*.

A short while later, Bibi Jeeuni arrived and spoke, "Son, come on, it is time to go home now. The *sangat* are preparing to leave for the village."

"Mata ji, you head home. I wish to stay within the *hazoori* of the Guru. I have this desire to read and learn here in Anandpur and earn the title of Khalsa. You head home with the others."

Deep Singh gave this response to his loving mother. Although he was content with family life, something had changed within him since arriving within the Guru's Darbar.

"Son, becoming a Singh one does not forget about their household duties and responsibilities," said Bibi Jeeuni before coming close and sitting beside him.

"Mata ji, it is not that I am trying to neglect or run away from my duties at home. I love you and family life, but at this moment, my heart wishes to stay here. I do not want to leave Anandpur; something is anchoring my body on this sacred land of the Guru."

Mother and son continued to converse before Guru Gobind Singh came over, having wished farewell to the *sangat* that was leaving. They both stood up and greeted the Guru.

"So, Deep Singh, you are heading back?" asked the Guru.

"Maharaj, he does not want to leave. He wants to remain here in Anandpur," said Bibi Jeeuni.

The Guru smiled. They looked towards Deep Singh and lovingly spoke, "Yes, leave him here. After all, his name is Deep; he will find the oil and spark a light for many in this world. Countless other deeps will be lit, oh, dear mother, leave him here in Anandpur."

No one is worthy of returning the Guru's *hukam*. Bibi Jeeuni and Bhai Bhagtu agreed and set off for their village, leaving Deep Singh in Anandpur.

Deep Singh had already begun to read and write Gurmukhi from a young age. In a short while, his *likhai,* that is his writing technique, developed into a beautiful calligraphy in praise of the Guru. Deep Singh slowly began to learn more Gurbani off by heart, lovingly reciting the Guru's Word, day and night. He learnt *shastar vidhia* and *ghor-svai,* the art of weaponry and horse riding. Two years passed like this in which time Deep Singh became a learned scholar and warrior. The Guru would take Deep Singh with them on hunting trips.

"Singho! The next few years are going to be very trying and tough for us all. We will be engaged in many battles against those who have set their eyes on Anandpur Sahib. We may even have to leave to continue growing and building this Panth of Guru Nanak Sahib. There will be much hardship to endure, many will become *shaheed,* and many more will need to regroup and live in the jungles to survive. You must uplift one another and keep your dharam and *rehat.* Akal Purakh will be your support."

Deep Singh listened to every word of the Guru and fully accepted the *hukam.* He turned to an older Singh with whom he had become very close and nodded to greet him.

"Are you ready for the road ahead, Singh ji?" asked Deep Singh.

"Even if the north star moved and the world shifted off its axis, a Sikh of the Guru could never waver from the Guru's *hukam.* With the blessings of Satguru, yes, Deep Singh ji, I am ready," replied the one they all called Mani Singh.

*****

"Baba Deep Singh met Bhai Mani Singh!?" Nihaal couldn't contain himself.

"Yes, son. Baba Deep Singh learnt from Bhai Mani Singh, and he would've had interactions with the Sahibzade, too, the Guru's sons."

"Wow!! How amazing it would have been to live in Anandpur Sahib then. So many amazing Gursikhs."

"And he took Amrit from the hands of Guru Gobind Singh!?" added Jeet.

"This is the glory of the Guru's Darbar that so many diamonds were forged during those days," Bibi Rano continued.

6.

It was early spring of 1701. The stars shone bright in the night sky as *Amrit Vela* arrived. The *manmukhs*, egoists, were in a deep sleep; however, the Gurmukhs and the *sants* were awake, in deep remembrance of their beloved Creator. Blessed are those souls who rise in the early hours to meditate on Vaheguru.

Deep Singh, too, was awake and sat cross-legged on the open veranda of a *bunga* in the hills of Anandpur Sahib. His eyes were closed with a *mala,* rosary beads, in his left hand, and a *khanda* that lay in its scabbard close to his right hand. He was emerged in s*imran*. This was part of his daily s*adhana*, spiritual discipline.

Deep Singh had full faith in the support of Akal Purakh, as he experienced much bliss during his s*imran*. Upon completing his *nitnem,* morning prayers, and *simran*, he stood up and began his *ardas* with a very particular thought in mind.

He stood with his hands tightly clasped in front of him, like those great warriors who had stood before major battles. With full attention and a pure mind, Deep Singh freely recited Gurbani, seeking the blessings of Akal

Purakh. He moved effortlessly, linking various *shabads* from Guru Granth Sahib and Dasam Granth. Imbued with love and bliss, in one breath, he exclaimed, "Vaheguru."

Deep Singh completed his *Ardas* and then made his way to the Guru. He wrapped a *lohi*, brown silk shawl, around himself but kept his hand on the hilt of his khanda, which hung around his torso. As he neared the Guru's Darbar, he could hear the melodious sound of Raag Kirtan emanating from the stringed instruments. He bowed to Guru Gobind Singh and took a seat at the front of the *divan*. Sitting in *sangat* to recite Gurbani together was the most blissful of experiences.

As day broke, many got up and headed back to their rooms to rest. Deep Singh stayed in the Darbar. He had heard Kavi Sainapati was going to relay the Battle of Bhangani 1688 that morning, which he had recorded for his work Sri Gur Sobha. Others came and joined Deep Singh. Guru Gobind Singh gave Kavi Sainapati the *agaya,* and he began to recite what he had recorded.

Deep Singh listened as Kavi Sainapati described the battleground. There was a fortress on the banks of the Yamuna River, where Singhs clad in iron and blue dresses were preparing for the battle. In the distance, an army led by Fateh Shah, King of Sri Nagar, was heading towards the fortress, named Paonta Sahib. They stopped and encamped some kilometres outside; a single horseman then rode across to Poanta Sahib. He exchanged words with a Singh

43

who had ridden in from the right. Both men then turned around and headed into their own camps. The Singh galloped back and bowed in front of Guru Gobind Singh, standing with a beautiful white hawk perched on his shoulder. As Kavi Sainapati spoke, the entire battle played out in front of Deep Singh's eyes.

After the Singh delivered his message, Guru Gobind Singh mounted his blue horse and marched to the battlefield with Nishaan Sahibs hoisted high above. Upon reaching the battlefield, Guru Sahib examined the enemy's positions and then deployed his Misls to take up their places around the enemy.

There were, in fact, eleven Misls under the command of Guru Gobind Singh, five of whom were headed up by the Guru's own cousins; Sango Shah, Jitmal, Sangat Rai, and Hari Chand – sons of Bibi Viro (the sister of Guru Tegh Bahudur). Gulab Rai, great-grandson of Guru Hargobind Sahib, was the head of a fifth Misl. Five further Misls were under the command of Pir Budhu Shah and his four sons, and the eleventh Misl was under the direct command of Guru Gobind Singh. The formation of the Misls was such that Guru Gobind Singh led from the centre, with his five cousins leading their units from the right wing, and Pir Budhu Shah and his sons leading the left wing.

Kavi Sainapati also named those on the Guru's side, the Guru's maternal uncle Kirpal Das, and Lal Chand, the son of Bidhi Chand, the beloved Gursikh of Guru Hargobind Sahib.

Fateh Shah of Sri Nagar was joined by other prominent Hindu Hill Chiefs such as Hari Chand Handooria and Bhim Chand of Bilaspur, as well as Mughal troops under Najabat Khan and Bhikham Khan.

Nagaray were played, the *narsingha* was blown, battle standards raised, and the Guru entered the battlefield. On the other side, Fateh Shah, having deployed his armed forces, stood firm and confident of victory. Beside him stood some of the most feared generals of the Hindu Hill Chiefs. In an instant, his forces began their charge towards the Guru and his Singhs. Both sides wielded their weapons and clashed most spectacularly. It was complete carnage as heads rolled from the first impact. The Guru's right flank was the most ferocious, pouncing on Fateh Shah's men like lions attacking their prey. Brandishing their swords, they pierced through many warriors. As a moth hovers around a lamp, unafraid of being struck down, such was the manner of the Singhs' movements. On one side, a Singh sliced a rival's body in two before cutting those pieces into four.

Another Singh on the right flank battled similarly, wielding his sword hard and fast. As he struck a blow on the approaching rider's head, he threw the sliced body to the ground. As he made mincemeat of the sliced bodies, he created such awe and terror on the battlefield that there was instant desertion from the enemy. That Singh of the Guru was acknowledged as the messenger of death on the battlefield.

In this manner, those ferocious Singhs, under the command of the Guru's cousins, continued to wreak havoc upon Fateh Shah's men. Deep Singh listened as Kavi Sainapati narrated how another wide-eyed Singh launched a barrage of arrows, which plunged into an entire enemy battalion. Cries of desperation were heard from Fateh Shah's side as many of his troops met the wrath of Guru Gobind Singh's warriors. Corpses upon corpses were piled up in heaps, and fountains of blood burst forth from the dead bodies.

Kirpal Das, the Guru's maternal uncle, routed out the famed Hayat Khan and killed him with a mighty blow. Other bodies were seen flying before falling into a gorge on the side. Fateh Shah's men had never encountered such warriors; even as they outnumbered the Guru's forces, they were overwhelmed by the Singhs, who encircled them like swarming locusts taking to a field of crops.

As the battle raged through its first phase, some of the Guru's faithful were struck with blows. With dagger in hand, Nand Chand carved through the enemy but was struck with a mighty blow. He fell to the ground, wounded, but was saved by the Guru. Despite the losses, the Guru's brave warriors battled on. Sango Shah was seen displaying such great feats of bravery that his actions were more daring than even the greatest warriors in Mahabharat. The arrogant and ego-fuelled soldiers who had arrived under Fateh Shah were routed by the prowling lions who charged through the battlefield.

Kavi Sainapati then explained how Jitmal attained martyrdom at the hands of Hari Chand, the Hindu Hill Chief of Handoor. Sango Shah, who had fought so valiantly was also martyred just after he killed Najabat Khan, the Pathan who had deserted Guru Gobind Singh's army before this battle. Sango Shah was later renamed Shah Sangram, the 'Monarch of War,' by Guru Gobind Singh for his acts of valour and bravery.

With two of the Guru's cousins and commanders of the right flanks falling, the Guru unleashed his wrath. Firing a barrage of arrows, he killed Bhikan Khan, another Pathan deserter. Hari Chand then re-entered the battle. He strung an arrow upon his bow and fired towards the Guru. The arrow missed but was shortly followed by another, which scraped off the Guru's steel body armour. Guru Gobind Singh then loaded his bow and fired a barrage of arrows towards Hari Chand. The Hill Chief of Handoor was instantly killed alongside two of his generals.

Following this decisive blow, the remaining combatants of Fateh Shah's army deserted the field. Trumpets of victory sounded from the Guru's camp. Deep Singh saw Kavi Sainapati smile as he narrated how a wave of joy spread amongst the Guru's faithful; they encircled the Guru and roared battle cries of victory:

"Bole So Nihal, Sat Sri Akal!!"

This was the Guru's first battle, and echoes of victory reverberated across the Darbar and throughout the three worlds.

Deep Singh sat for a while longer, conversing with the Singhs, some of whom had seen the Khalsa in battle. Even though Deep Singh had spent two years at Anandpur Sahib, he was yet to witness the fighting prowess of the Khalsa, but he learned a lot from listening to those who had.

7.

During those days in Anandpur Sahib, the Panth grew in numbers as many took Amrit and became Khalsa. Besides meaning pure in Sanskrit, the word Khalsa is a Persian term meaning free or autonomous. Historically it was the term used for a particular section of land under the direct control and ownership of the Mughal emperor. All revenue contributions from this type of land were sent directly to the Mughal treasury without interference from the Jagirdars or revenue collectors. The use of the term Khalsa by Guru Gobind Singh was a direct challenge to Mughal power and authority; it was reminiscent of Guru Amar Das' decision to create 22 Manjhis to reflect the 22 states under Mughal rule. It was the creation of a parallel power structure, one which reported directly to the Guru, safe from the deceitful ways of the Masands, to enhance the sovereignty and authority of the Guru's Darbar.

Deep Singh was sitting amongst the sangat of Gursikhs. Bhai Mani Singh was speaking about the Vaisakhi of 1699.

"Guru Gobind Singh decentralised and delegated their temporal power to the Khalsa and placed them in positions of power in every sphere of activity."

Another Singh added to this.

"Following the creation of the Khalsa, Guru Gobind Singh deployed the newly appointed emissaries in all four directions. From Anandpur Sahib, Guru Sahib travelled to Amritsar and Patna and several other places of the Guru Darbar's influence. Considering the influence of Masands, this was a bold and revolutionary new move designed to oust the corrupt Masands and re-establish the sanctity and sovereignty of the Guru's Darbar. Armed with *panj-kakkar*, the young Gursikhs were dispatched with full powers to initiate others into the Khalsa Panth."

*****

"Bibi Rano ji, but I learnt in school that the *panj-kakkar* worn by the Khalsa are articles of faith," Jeet interjected.

Bibi Rano smiled before explaining, "That is what we are taught today in schools, *puth*, but that is not what the *panj-kakkar* are."

"What are they?" asked Nihaal.

"Well, from the writings of pre-colonial texts, we find that the significance of administering Amrit was that it was an initiation ceremony, not a baptism that carries a Christian connotation. The creation of the Khalsa was about empowering the individual Sikh to oppose falsehood, tyranny, and oppression. That empowerment came directly from the Guru as they bestowed sovereignty on each Sikh, and the Khalsa collective, before kneeling and asking for Amrit too.

"Guru Gobind Singh assigned such symbols to every member of the Khalsa that they became a living insignia, distinguishable from a distance, of the open revolution Guru Sahib had launched. It was a direct confrontation between Khalsa and the Imperial regime. There were no illusions on either side; the Sikhs knew there could be no compromise between their revolution and the established order it was mandated to overthrow."

"What is a precolo …" Nihaal stumbled with his words.

"Precolonial means the time before the British arrived in Panjab and took over. That happened in 1849, over one-hundred-and-seventy years ago," explained Bibi Rano.

Nihaal and Jeet looked at one another. Sensing that was a lesson for another day, Bibi Rano continued with the story.

"Ordinarily, the *panj-kakkar* are known as Kes, uncut hair; Kanga, comb; Kachera, undergarment; Kirpan, a dagger, and Kara, an iron bracelet. However, the precolo–, the Sikh accounts that we have before the British arrived in Panjab, narrate that the five main attributes of the Khalsa were Kes, Kanga, Kachera, Kard, and the love for weapons and Shabad. There is no mention of Kara. Perhaps because historically, a Kara would've been considered a weapon for both offensive and defensive use, falling within the broader instruction of bearing arms."

Nihaal and Jeet continued to listen as Bib Rano returned to Anandpur Sahib.

*****

Bhai Mani Singh was still speaking.

"Following the creation of the Khalsa, there was strong opposition from both the Mughal regime and Hindu Hill Rajas and some of the Sikh followers who had not quite shaken off the stranglehold of the Brahmanical caste order."

Deep Singh and others learned about the importance of Khalsa Rehat, discipline, both as a means of actualizing the ideals and conduct of the Khalsa and as an identifying characteristic of the Khalsa.

"The creation of the Khalsa and its immediate deployment all over the land saw a radical expansion of the Sikh Panth; however, Guru Sahib's headquarters remained in Anandpur Sahib." Bhai Mani Singh paused and looked out over the, hills of Anandpur before continuing, "As you all know, a couple of years ago, the Hill Chief of Kahloor claimed the land of Anandpur Sahib was his to take and threatened to wage war with the Guru if he did not vacate the territory. The Guru chose to remain in Anandpur Sahib and duly accepted the challenge. This decision carried an incredibly important lesson for Sikhs: that this territory belongs to the Guru's Darbar, to the Guru's Khalsa, and we had every intention of defending our territory."

"This was the battle in which Sahibzada Baba Ajit Singh first displayed exemplary courage and great military prowess in the clash that lasted four whole days, resulting in victory for the Guru's forces. Unable to penetrate the Guru's forces defending from the seven forts at Anandpur Sahib, the Hill Rajas retreated but soon hatched a plan to send an intoxicated elephant to break down the barricade outside Fort Lohgarh. However, they were met by the Guru's brave and courageous Khalsa, including the legendary Bhai Bachittar Singh, who delivered a fatal blow to the charging intoxicated elephant. The Khalsa remained victorious, and the Hill Rajas were forced to retreat once again. They suffered some large blows in this series of battles, including the death of Raja Kesri Chand, whose head was severed by the sword of Bhai Uday Singh before he presented it at the feet of Gurū Gobind Singh."

Deep Singh listened as Bhai Mani Singh expanded on the importance of preserving and defending sovereign Sikh land.

"With no other option left, the Hill Rajas led by Raja Ajmer Chand, met and consoled one another. They drafted a letter, tied it to a cow, and left it outside the Fort of Anandgarh. In the letter, they acknowledged their mistakes and swore on the cow, whom they deemed holy, and the Hindu sacred thread that they would never raid Anandpur Sahib again. They also lamented that they were ashamed to show their faces to the hill people, but if the Guru left the Fort of Anandgarh just once and returned later, it would help them restore some dignity."

One of the *langari sevadars* arrived with cool *lassi* and served it to the Sangat, who remained fixated as Bhai Mani Singh continued. Deep Singh got up to help with serving but continued to listen.

"Guru Sahib did not trust their oaths of swearing on the cow or Hindu sacred thread but accepted their mercy petition. The Guru moved to a hilltop in the valley of Nirmoh, just south of Kīratpur. However, the moment Guru Sahib and the Khalsa forces retreated, the Hindu Hill Rajas broke all their pledges and took occupation of all the villages surrounding Anandpur Sahib. Raja Ajmer Chand addressed the other Hill Rajas and conspired to attack the Guru and Khalsa forces at Nirmoh, whom he thought would not be able to defend themselves without the protection of any fort.

"The plan was to surround Guru Sahib, kill or capture them, and present them to the Mughal Suba of Sirhind. Some of the Hill Rajas did not agree to the plan; however, the majority felt it was the best course of action to cement their control and influence over the region. They attacked

Nirmoh on 8th October 1700; however, they met firm resistance from the Guru's encampment."

Bhai Mani Singh paused as Kavi Sainapati arrived to take a seat.

"We were just remembering the time Raja Ajmer Chand betrayed the Guru," he said.

"You are the Guru's Court poet; please, continue the account, Kavi ji." Bhai Mani Singh clasped his hands and shuffled back.

Kavi Sainapati sat down cross-legged and continued, "They were ill-prepared. Unable to penetrate Sikh fortifications, Raja Ajmer Chand, the son of Bhim Chand, sent a letter through his Minister Parma Nand to the Governor of Sirhind, asking for back-up forces to be deployed. The Mughal Governor sent Rustam Khan, who, if you recall, was the commander who had failed to break through the Guru's forces at Anandpur five years earlier. As it transpired, the Governor of Sirhind, in choosing to send Rustam Khan, had effectively signed his death warrant as an arrow fired by the Guru killed him, and his brother Nasir Ali Khan was killed similarly by an arrow fired by the Guru's formidable General, Bhai Uday Singh."

"Dhan Guru Dhan Guru Pyar-e," said one of the Singhs.

Another one let out a loud *jakara*.

Kavi Sainapati continued, "This was only the second battle of the Khalsa, but the seventh time Guru Gobind Singh had led the Sikh warriors into battle. There were three further encounters with the Hindu Hill Chiefs before the Guru returned to Anandpur Sahib in late 1700. Upon returning to Anandpur Sahib, Guru Sahib initiated a phase of fortifying the territory that had become a citadel of Sikh power. Anandpur Sahib was turned into a town of bliss with its inhabitants singing of the glory that prevailed at Anandpur."

Kavi Sainapati's unique portrayal of Guru Sahib's victorious battles shed much light on the expansive rise of Sikh power under Guru Gobind Singh ji. From the initial challenges of Guru Nanak Sahib to the martyrdom of Guru Arjan Sahib, the powerbrokers of South Asia were conscious of the growing rise of the Sikh movement. Ever since Guru Hargobind Sahib's decision to adorn two swords, one representing rule over the temporal and one over the spiritual, which represented the next phase of Guru Nanak Sahib's revolution, the Mughal empire began to feel the effects of Sikh warfare, and that was extended to the Hill Rajas. The manner with which Guru Sahib galvanised the Sikhs following the martyrdom of Guru Tegh Bahadur Sahib, the second such ordeal the Sikhs endured that century, speaks volumes about the Guru's radiant glory and captivating appeal.

The sangat spent the rest of the morning listening to the accounts from Bhai Mani Singh and Kavi Sainapati. Deep Singh was in high spirits. He listened to other accounts before heading over to the open grounds where the Khalsa were training.

"Ajo Deep Singh ji."

Deep Singh looked up to see Bhai Daya Singh's beaming smile.

"Sat Kartar."

"Akaal hi Akaal."

The two Gursikhs embraced. Deep Singh bowed before the Guru, picked up his *shaster*, and began his *pentra*.

This is how the Khalsa would spend their time in Anandpur Sahib during that period of relative peace. The mornings would usually start with *kirtan* and *katha*, followed by some learning from the Guru's Court poets such as Kavi Sainapat, and listening to the wise words of Gursikhs, such as Bhai Mani Singh. The afternoons were spent on physical training and hunting.

8.

It was the winter months of 1709. Thousands of Sikhs had gathered in Kiratpur Sahib in anticipation of Banda Singh Bahadur's arrival. Many had heard about his movement from the south but had not seen him in person. They were excited to meet the Sikh, who had been hand-picked by the Guru to lead the Khalsa as an equal amongst the Khalsa.

Some had questioned how a former *bairagi,* ascetic, could move with such military precision and efficiency that was often only possible by a seasoned warrior.

"I've heard he has superpowers," said one of the villagers.

"I've heard he was part of a Sikh regiment in the Mughal army," said another.

Overhearing the commotion, an older Singh stepped into the circle and spoke,

"No, no! His superpower is the Panj-Pyar-e that the Guru assigned to him."

"What do you mean, brother?" asked the first man.

"Well, we cannot ignore the influence of the Panj, who are travelling with Banda Singh. They are some of the most battle-hardened warriors who served under the Guru. They know the terrain, and the Guru's instruction to Banda Singh last year was always to seek the wise counsel of the Panj."

The small crowd that had gathered acknowledged those words in unison.

"I never thought of that," said the first man. "What is your name, Khalsa ji?" he asked.

"Hardas," came the reply.

Baba Hardas Singh was a writer who had spent time with the Guru at Anandpur Sahib. He was very well respected and one of a handful of *hazoori* Singhs that remained. He had answered Banda Singh's call, which had arrived a few months earlier, and amassed the large gathering at Kiratpur Sahib, where final preparations were to be made before the march on Sirhind.

Deep Singh had also made his way to Kiratpur Sahib with a *jatha* of Sikhs from Majha. He had set up camp and was seeing to the horses when he heard someone behind him.

"Vaheguru ji ka Khalsa Vaheguru ji ki Fateh Deep Singh!"

Deep Singh turned around to see the large frame of Baba Hardas Singh standing with open arms. The two Gursikhs immediately embraced,

"Vaheguru ji ka Khalsa Vaheguru ji ki Fateh Baba ji!" replied Deep Singh.

The two had not seen each other since the Siege of Anandpur five years ago.

"*Dhan bhag sadde*, I am blessed. To have your darshan again, how have you been, Baba ji?" asked Deep Singh.

"*Chardikala, Maharaj kirpa,*" replied Baba Hardas Singh.

The two sat down and caught up on the happenings of the past few years. As they spoke, many more Sikhs arrived from across Majha and Doaba. The area was soon overflowing with Sikhs dressed in blue and yellow. Tents were pitched up, and the horses were seen to. A large langar was prepared with *sevadars* hurriedly attending to the *sangat*.

"Have you received any further message about Banda Singh's arrival?" Deep Singh asked Baba Hardas Singh.

"No. the instruction from Jathedar was to await the arrival of his *jatha*. No one is to take any steps towards

Sirhind until they arrive. I know the Khalsa here are eager to march on Sirhind and deliver Khalsai justice to the likes of Wazir Khan and Sucha Nand, but the Jathedar's *hukam* is to wait," Baba Hardas Singh explained.

"I heard they had passed Sadhaura and taken care of Osman Khan," said Deep Singh.

"Yes, the one who had burned alive Pir Buddhu Shah for his alliance with the Guru's Darbar. The Jathedar is taking no prisoners; the response of the Khalsa is swift and precise," replied Baba Hardas Singh.

"Baba ji, I heard about Bahadur Shah's betrayal. Even after Guru Gobind Singh ji killed Tara Azam in the Battle of Jajau a couple of years ago, he reneged out of his agreement with the Guru and made excuses," Deep Singh said.

"Hanji, yes, that is correct. The Guru and Khalsa put Bahadur Shah on the throne, but he did not keep his end of the deal. The Guru had given him a list of names to hand over to the Khalsa, which included the likes of Wazir Khan, but Bahadur Shah had said he needed time, five to seven years, to cement his position as the emperor, and then he would hand them over to the Khalsa," Baba Hardas Singh explained.

Although Deep Singh had spent time with the Guru at Damdama Sahib, helping Bhai Mani Singh with the compilation of Guru Granth Sahib, the Guru had moved down south soon after. There had been no direct communication between the Guru and Deep Singh after that moment.

"When Bahadur Shah reneged on his promise, the Guru told him he would send his own *banda*, his own man, who would deliver justice for the Khalsa. *Dhan Guru Kalgidhar Pita, Dhan Guru ke pyar-e,*" Baba Hardas Singh continued.

The two Gursikhs continued to catch up on events for several hours. A little while later, a messenger arrived to say Banda Singh and the Khalsa were now en route to Banur, and the Khalsa that had gathered at Kiratpur Sahib was to start making its way to Kharur. This was the message everyone was waiting for. In an instant, the ever-ready Khalsa gathered with their horses. Deep Singh assembled his *jatha*. Baba Hardas Singh assembled the Singhs that had come with him.

Soon after setting off for Ropar, Baba Hardas Singh's *jatha* clashed with a contingent of Mughals headed up by Nawab Sher Muhammad of Malerkotla, where the Battle of Ghumsan took place. Sher Muhammed's brothers Khizar Khan, Nastar Khan, and Vali Muhammed Khan were killed by the Khalsa. Sher Muhammed himself was injured. The Singhs pushed back the blockade and marched forward.

From the other side, Banda Singh Bahadur had reached the outskirts of Sirhind. Most of the surrounding towns around Sirhind had fallen into the hands of the Khalsa. Banda Singh's Khalsa met with the large *jatha* of Khalsa warriors who had travelled under Baba Hardas Singh and Deep Singh from Majha and Doaba.

A large Gurmatta was convened between the Jathedars. This was the first major meeting of Qaumi Jathedars since Guru Gobind Singh ji had departed this world. The atmosphere was electric as Sikhs gathered around the inner circle that had formed. Within the circle, to the left of Banda Singh sat Bhai Baaj Singh, Bhai Karam Singh, Bhai Dharam Singh, Bhai Aali Singh, Bhai Mali Singh, Bhai Sangram Singh, Bhai Mehtab Singh, and Giani Bhagvan Singh. To the right of Banda Singh sat Baba Binod Singh and Baba Hardas Singh. Deep Singh took his place next to Baba Hardas Singh. Next to him sat Bhai Bajjar Singh, Bhai Fateh Singh, Bhai Sham Singh, Bhai Bir Singh, and Bhai Ran Singh.

The Jathedars clasped their hands, and a thundering Fateh followed.

"Vaheguru ji ka Khalsa Vaheguru ji ki Fateh."

"Dhan Guru Kalgiawale, all praise to the Wearer of the Royal Plume," Banda Singh spoke.

Seated in *bir-asan*, the warrior pose, he was cladded in navy blue *bana* and chainmail. The quiver of arrows handed to him by Guru Gobind Singh ji was wrapped around his body. His right hand was placed firmly on the hilt of his sword, and in his left hand, he moved a *mala,* rosary.

Deep Singh was sat in a *chaunkra*, cross-legged, with his Khanda lying across his lap. The other Jathedars were seated similarly, forming a powerful circle of blue and iron-clad warriors.

9.

Nihaal and Jeet had been sitting for a while, and although they were eager to return to the episode Bibi Rano had started with, namely the *hukam* from the Dal Khalsa, this was the meeting that Nihaal had been looking forward to learning about all week. His mind was racing with anticipation of what was about to happen.

Bibi Rano continued the story.

*****

The Jathedars began by discussing the number of enemy troops that awaited them in Sirhind. While the troops in Sirhind were more in number, the larger concern for them was Sirhind's greater firepower. Wazir Khan, the Mughal governor, had large cannons, artillery guns, an assortment of rifles, ample gunpowder, and bullets, a large battalion of elephants, and many battalions of horses under his command. The Khalsa did not have cannons or large artillery guns, nor did they have a battalion of elephants.

65

Their horses were also fewer in number, with most of the Khalsa army on foot. Their arsenal was mainly comprised of rifles, bows and arrows, an assortment of swords, spears, and other handheld close combat weapons.

"Our greatest weapon is the desire to avenge the death of the *Sahibzade*, to deliver Khalsai justice to those blood-thirsty oppressors who killed the Guru's beloved sons and establish Khalsa Raj," Deep Singh heard Baba Hardas Singh speak.

"We have arrived here with only one thought in mind, that the Khalsa will liberate Sirhind even if it means we lose our own lives," he continued.

Like a wise general, Banda Singh Bahadur was listening to the thoughts of all the Jathedars who individually expressed similar views. Despite the passionate speeches from those around him, Banda Singh Bahadur remained seated in *bir-asan*, continuing to move the *mala* through his hand.

The Jathedars spoke about the makeup of the Khalsa army. In addition to the committed warriors, they recognised that there was a group of paid Sikhs soldiers sent by local leaders in Malwa and another group comprised of disgruntled Hindus and Muslims who had left Sirhind to join the Khalsa forces. Acknowledging this, the Jathedars understood the potential risk of these latter groups deserting the Khalsa if it appeared the forces in Sirhind were gaining the upper hand.

The Jathedars read the *hukamnama* that Guru Gobind Singh ji sent with Banda Singh and affirmed their commitment to fulfilling every word of the Guru. Deep Singh then watched on as Banda Singh addressed the Jathedars:

"Khalsa ji, approximately five years earlier, the Guru's beloved young *Sahibzade* were bricked alive in Sirhind. That moment marked the beginning of the end of the Mughal regime. We have been travelling up from the south with Guru's Kirpa. The Khalsa has liberated many towns, and now we shall raze Sirhind to the ground before liberating its people. We shall punish those who attacked the Guru's Darbar and betrayed the Guru. Those who committed the heinous act of killing the Guru's young *Sahibzade and destroying many more lives* will not be spared. They will feel the full force of the Khalsa. We have instructions to establish Halemi Raj. With the support of Akal Purakh and the blessings of the Guru, the Khalsa shall be victorious. If *shaheedi* awaits us in Sirhind, then we will embrace it and enter *Sach Khand* to the resounding echo of *jakaray.* Either way, Sirhind's tyrants will feel the Khalsa's full force."

"kushia de jakaray gajave nihaal ho jaave kalgidhar patshah de man nu pave sat sri akaal," came a deafening *jakara* from Bhai Binod Singh.

"hum rakhat patshahi dava, ja itt ko ja aglo pava, je satgur sikhan kahi baat hog saee nahi khali jaat!" Baba Hardas Singh

spoke of the Khalsa's desire to establish Raj, that if it is not established in this life, then it will be established by the Khalsa in the next!

Bhai Baaj Singh was dressed in a dark blue *chola* with a tall *dumalla* and *farla.* His whole body was draped in an assortment of weapons – *swords, katars, chakars, tabars and teers* –a one-man army ready to uproot the Mughal regime. Deep Singh observed as Bhai Baaj Singh spoke in a deep raspy voice:

"We sit together here in praise of Satguru Sache Patshah Sahib Sri Guru Nanak Dev ji Maharaj, the Emperor of emperors, the true sovereign of both worlds."

Deep Singh noticed the fresh battle scar that ran down Bhai Baaj Singh's face. Rare was the sight of such fearless Singhs. *Only the sangat of the Gurmukhs creates such chardikala warriors*, thought Deep Singh.

Bhai Baaj Singh continued:

"We seek only the *agaya* of that *jot* of Nanak-Gur Gobind Singh, that brings the immaculate liberating wisdom of *nam.* With the Guru by our side, the Khalsa can shift the world off its axis, such is the power of *amrit* that sparrows turn to hawks and hunt down those who prey on the innocent. The immortal victory of Sache Patshah Sahib Sri Guru Nanak Dev ji Maharaj guarantees the success of the Khalsa!"

There was an electric atmosphere as Deep Singh continued to listen to shouts of *"raj karega khalsa"* and *"panth ki jeet"!* He looked towards Baba Hardas Singh, then towards the others sitting in the *Gurmatta,* including Bhai Sangram Singh, the son of Shaheed Bhai Bachhitar Singh. Next to him sat Bhai Mehtab Singh and Bhai Fateh Singh, the sons of Shaheed Bhai Uday Singh. All three loudly reciprocated the proclamations of *"raj karega khalsa"* that emanated around them. A little further up, he saw the young *gatka ustad* Bhai Bajjar Singh who stood up following Bhai Baaj Singh's riling speech and raised his fists.

Bhai Binod Singh then stood up and addressed the Gurmatta:

"Every single Sikh present here today pledges to deliver on the *hukam* of the Guru – *asur sangharbe ko durjan ke marbe ko, sankat nivarbe ko Khalsa banayo hai* – the Guru created the Khalsa to eradicate the world's suffering by always striving to decimate the demonic forces and annihilate them from the face of this earth. We collectively pledge our commitment to that objective, not to stop until the sovereign flags of the Guru Khalsa Panth fly in Sirhind and all over the land of the five rivers. We shall not rest until the Khalsa achieves its goal."

Hearing this, many more raised their fists high towards the sky. Deep Singh looked towards Banda Singh, who slowly stood up, acknowledged Deep Singh, placed his *mala* hand on the shoulder of Bhai Binod Singh, and then folded his hands in reverence to the Singhs.

The Jathedars made their final preparations for the march towards Sirhind. The atmosphere was one Deep Singh had not experienced before, but he thanked Akal Purakh for this moment. He had not been with the Khalsa during the Battle of Chamkaur Sahib or Mukhtsar Sahib, but he was here with them now and was fully committed to deliver on the *hukam* of the Guru.

The Jathedars gathered their units and initiated their march towards Sirhind, slowly picking up pace. Within a few minutes, the large convoy of Khalsa warriors, led by Banda Singh Bahadur, were galloping at full speed to change the course of history forever.

Elsewhere, approximately twelve *koh* outside of Sarhind, Wazir Khan had assembled his forces in the open fields of Chapparchiri. His cannons and heavy artillery units were stationed at the front, with various units of elephants and horses behind them. Tens of thousands had gathered to withstand the storm that was about to be unleashed by the Khalsa.

The first sight of Khalsai *jhande* triggered the Mughal forces into firing their cannons. A barrage of heavy fire was launched towards the advancing Singhs. As predicted by the Jathedars, those empty vessels that had filled their bags with the loot from Samana, Sadhaura, Mustafabad, Kapuri, and other towns, deserted the Khalsa the moment they heard the deafening sound of cannon fire.

The *sidhaki* Khalsa remained resolute, venturing directly towards the cannon fire. Thick black smoke rose into the air after the cannonballs hit the ground. The resolute Khalsa did not look back; their focus was firmly on the enemy troops in front of them spread out across Chapparchiri. Bhai Baaj Singh, Bhai Binod Singh, Baba Hardas Singh, and Deep Singh were leading their units, flanking the main convoy led by the general, Banda Singh Bahadur. As they neared the small mounds upon where the cannons had been placed, they reached for the hilts of their swords and spread them out like the wings of a hawk preparing to swoop down on its prey. As the Khalsa neared the line of cannons, Banda Singh Bahadur reached for one of the five arrows given to him by Guru Gobind Singh ji in Nanded. He swiftly placed it upon his bow, strung back with an almighty pull, and let it fly towards the larger cannon in the centre of the Mughal defence line. The arrow whistled past the Khalsa, who were swooping down on the cannons. It struck directly into the main cannon, causing a mighty explosion. The sky lit up; those Mughals stationed at the remaining cannons met their death in the swiftest manner as the Khalsa swords sliced through their bodies without their horses breaking pace.

The Khalsa entered Chapparchiri with such speed that multiple Mughal bodies were severed instantly. Bolts of lightning came raining down as the sword-swinging Khalsa adorned in their electric blue *bana* cut through the first Mughal defence. Wazir Khan was stationed a mile back but watched with unease at the ferocity and speed with which Kalgidhar Patshah's Khalsa annihilated his men.

Bhai Binod Singh, Bhai Baaj Singh, Bhai Fateh Singh, Bhai Aali Singh, Bhai Mali Singh, Baba Hardas Singh, Deep Singh, Bhai Sangram Singh, Giani Bhagvan Singh, Bhai Mehtab Singh, Baba Bir Singh, Bhai Karam Singh, Bhai Dharam Singh, and Bhai Bajjar Singh all advanced their units, and clashing with Wazir Khan's troops they made steady progress. The Khalsa swept across the Chapparchiri battlefield dyeing the ground red with the blood of Mughal troops.

The battle waged into the afternoon. By sunset, the two Mughal contingents on either side of Wazir Khan's battalion had been obliterated. Those Mughal troops who had entered Chapparchiri in the name of *jihad* had either fallen at the hands of the Khalsa or ran away from the battlefield. Nawab Sher Muhammad from Malerkotla had been slain, but Wazir Khan remained sitting atop his elephant, frantically shouting instructions to his troops. Then out of nowhere, an arrow was fired, which struck his elephant square in the head. This caused Wazir Khan to fall to the ground. Seeing this, many more Mughal troops dropped their weapons and ran away. The blood-soaked battlefield of Chapparchiri now fell into the overall command of the Khalsa.

Baba Hardas Singh was riddled with battle wounds, but he was still standing. He looked around but could not see those fighting near him, like Giani Bhagwan Singh, Bhai Sangram Singh, and Bhai Mehtab Singh. He saw a *jatha* of Singhs chasing the Mughal troops towards Sirhind and thought, *perhaps Bhagvan Singh and the others have advanced into Sirhind.* With that thought in mind, he jumped on his horse and pulled back the reins to head towards Sirhind. Moments later, he stopped his horse and looked around the battlefield. The sight of *shaheed* Singhs made him realise he could not leave the battlefield without first performing their final rites. He called over some of the Singhs on horseback, Bhai Baaj Singh, Bhai Kahan Singh, and Bhai Binod Singh were also still at Chapparchiri. Together they collected the *shaheed saroops* of the Singhs and formed a large *shaheedi ganj,* funeral pyre of the martyrs, before Bhai Binod Singh recited an *ardas* to complete their final rites. Approximately six thousand Singhs had attained shaheedi in the Battle of Chapparchiri (1709). The body count of the Mughal troops was close to three times this number.

Baba Hardas Singh also spotted the *shaheedi saroop* of Bhai Bajjar Singh, the *gatka ustad* who had trained many Gursikhs from Anandpur Sahib. He had taught Baba Hardas Singh and Deep Singh mainly difficult *pentras.* Bhai Bajjar Singh's family had served the Guru's House for generations. His grandfather, Shaheed Bhai Sukhia Rathor, was a general under Miri Piri de Malik Sri Guru Hargobind

Sahib ji Maharaj. He was also the *fuffar ji* of Bhai Mani Singh. Baba Hardas Singh also fondly remembered the brothers of Bhai Bajjar Singh, namely Bhai Jeeta Singh and Bhai Neta Singh, who had fought valiantly in many battles from Anandpur Sahib before they, too had attained *shaheedi*. Bhai Bajjar Singh's daughter, Bibi Bhikka had attained shaheedi during the Great Separation of Sirsa following the Siege of Anandpur. Her husband, Bhai Alam Singh, had attained *shaheedi* at the Battle of Chamkaur Sahib. Such was the commitment and sacrifice of the entire family towards the Guru and the Khalsa, that Bhai Bajjar Singh himself had not only raised and trained many who went on to attain *shaheedi* but following the hukam from Guru Gobind Singh ji, he had travelled with Banda Singh Bahadur from Nanded and taken his place amongst the thousands who currently rested their bodies at Chapparchiri. Just beside Bhai Bajjar Singh lay Bhai Sangram Singh, Bhai Mehtab Singh, and Bhai Fateh Singh, the three grandsons of Bhai Mani Singh.

As the *shaheed ganj* was lit, the Singhs also piled up the bodies of the Mughal troops and attended to wounded warriors from both sides. Wazir Khan was still breathing. Bhai Aali Singh and Bhai Mali Singh tied him to the back of their horses and dragged him all the way to Sirhind, where he was tied upside down in the tree for the eagles to feast on.

Elsewhere in Sirhind, Sucha Nand was pulled out of his hiding spot. His face was blackened, and he was paraded through the streets on the back of a donkey.

The Khalsa raised sovereign flags of the Guru Khalsa Panth across Sirhind. Banda Singh Bahadur addressed some locals and reassured them of the Khalsa's arrival. They were all thankful because the likes of Wazir Khan and Sucha Nand had brought them much grief and pain.

A Sarbat Khalsa was held in which Banda Singh Bahadur appointed certain administrative and leadership responsibilities to the likes of Bhai Binod Singh, Bhai Baaj Singh, Bhai Ram Singh, Bhai Fateh Singh, Bhai Sham Singh and Bhai Koer Singh.

Banda Singh Bahadur then turned and embraced Deep Singh, who had killed many enemy soldiers and kept the Khalsa in high spirits through the battle. He was bestowed with the honorific title of *jinda shaheed*, living martyr. The *jatha* of Singhs from Majha and Malwa let out roars of *jakaray,* which rung out all over Sirhind. Despite being one of the youngest at 27, Deep Singh received the respect of many battle-hardened warriors. Within a few days following the Sarbat Khalsa, the Khalsa took control of Saharanpur, Karnal, and Panipat. They renamed Fort Muklisgarh to Lohgarh, which became the Capital of the Sikhs as Banda Singh Bahadur established Khalsa Raj, minting coins in praise of the Great Gurus.

10.

1755 was a dark year for the towns and cities that linked Panjab to Delhi because Ahmad Shah Durrani, also known as Ahmad Shah Abdali, had invaded from Afghanistan for the fourth occasion, this time upon the intel provided by Mir Mannu's *begum*. He had a force of approximately seven thousand troops, but just like his previous invasions, he did not arrive with the intent to rule, only to loot and plunder and then return with the riches he had stolen.

The Mughal army in Delhi clashed with his forces but put up little resistance. They were never truly equipped to withstand the invasion as Abdali's men were greater in number and better fighters. Each Mughal checkpoint that led to the city suffered heavy casualties.

Abdali had first hit the towns of Mathara, then Bindraban, followed by a large hit on Magra. The Mughals were obliterated by Abdali's men who soon arrived in the city centre, where they had open access to the city's riches due to the army's inadequacy and the collusion of the *begum*.

The *begum* provided Abdali with the addresses of all the rich and influential people. They took expensive ornaments, fine cloths, gold, money, and many women and children. Whoever mustered a little courage to try and stop Abdali had their hands chopped off. If anyone dared to speak out against him, he had his men cut their tongues. Many innocent people were slaughtered in front of their families. Abdali did not differentiate between Hindu and Muslim; he pillaged and looted their properties. He specifically targeted young women aged between fifteen and twenty-five and young men aged eighteen to twenty-five. He took the entire city captive and then loaded the carts with the loot; thousands of bulls were lined up and loaded.

Some of Abdali's men came across a Muslim *pir* at home with his daughter-in-law and grandson. He pleaded with them, "Please, in Allah's name, do not take them. I will give you all my money."

As he returned with a small bag, the men laughed and snatched the bag off him before striking him down and taking the young woman and child. They dragged them outside and threw them onto the cart. Another person came along and dragged the mother away from her child as she kicked and screamed. The man slapped her until she fell unconscious and threw her onto another cart with women. Abdali's men were not God-fearing but animalistic and driven by worldly greed. They felt invincible and had little reason to doubt this because there was little to no resistance from anyone in Delhi.

Elsewhere a young family had been visiting the Mandir when Abdali's men grabbed them. The parents were beaten and thrown onto separate carts. Any little money or possessions on their persons was snatched and added to the carts of goods. The two young children were also separated and locked up in cages. They cried out for their parents to help free them, but they were in and out of consciousness.

Some of Abdali's men rounded a marketplace and ransacked all the tables, throwing to waste produce and carefully selected garments. Some managed to escape down the narrow streets that ran off the main square; others were not so lucky. A similar pattern of violence was inflicted upon those that were caught. They were beaten, separated, and thrown onto carts.

The Afghans and the Marathas had already looted Delhi. While immense wealth had been taken, including the koh-i-noor diamond and the famous peacock throne, there was still plenty of treasure for Abdali's men to find and loot. They loaded their carts with the immense treasures and continued to snatch young women and children.

Abdali had sat on the throne in the Delhi palace. The Mughal emperor of Delhi sat at his feet like a slave. The room was full of Abdali's men, each holding palace guards in front of them on their knees. Upon Abdali's order, the guards were beaten. As their bodies were broken, the emperor shrieked and closed his eyes.

"Someone tell me, is there any home in this city belonging to an *amir* that has not been raided?" asked Abdali.

One of his men answered:

"Alamgir Badshah, all of Delhi has been looted. We have cartloads of gold, fine cloth, and beautiful women to take back with us. The men and children have been rounded up too. No one has been able to put up any resistance to stop us."

"Very well," said Abdali stroking his short pointy white beard. His green eyes scanned the palace room until they stopped on a corner where some of the emperor's personal attendants were crouched together. He looked back down at the emperor and began to laugh.

"I have heard your daughter, Hazrat *begum*, is very beautiful. Is this true?"

The emperor looked up at Abdali but stopped short of saying anything. Abdali turned towards him and bellowed, "Well, have I heard right?"

The emperor lowered his gaze and bowed his head in submission, but Abdali was not in any mood for mercy.

"Bring her to me here. I order her to be wedded to me right away," replied Abdali.

The room fell silent. Abdali's words shook the emperor to his core. It was like the wind had stopped blowing outside, and the birds had stopped chirping. Before he knew it, two of Abdali's men lifted him off the ground and took him from the room.

"You heard the order, prepare Hazrat *begum* for her wedding," shouted another guard.

Some of the servants began to wail out and begged for it not to happen.

"She is just a child!" one screamed.

"Please let her be," another one added.

Their pleas were met with a barrage of slaps from the guards, who then dragged them out of the palace room. The rest of the room was also cleared, and preparations were made for the wedding that day.

"Does anyone else have anything to say?" asked Abdali.

There was brief silence until an old man towards the back of the room spoke:

"This is not Islam. You have been lured by *Iblis,* the devil! May Allah be your saviour."

Abdali turned towards where the man was sitting. With hands clenched behind his back, he started to walk over to him. The Pathan guards cleared his path, pushing back the Mughal court attendants that remained to one side. Abdali hovered over the old man and said, "I have been lured by *Iblis,* you say?"

The old man had been forced to his knees. He said nothing but looked up in defiance at Abdali square in the face.

"Look around you old man. The Mughals of Delhi are weak; they have been looted by Afghans and those *kafirs* from the south for decades! They need this lesson. They need to feel the wrath of my power to awaken them from their slumber!"

"They are God-fearing men, unlike you. They may not have the power to resist you, but Allah will send his messengers of truth. They will stop you," said the old man.

"Hahaha …" laughed Abdali. "And where are these messengers of truth you speak of? I have not seen any resistance from these weak people. They are not worthy of holding such wealth. I am here to relieve them of their duties."

The old man ran his prayer beads through his hands.

"When I came as a general under Nadir Shah, I saw first-hand how weak the Mughal leaders had become. This was inevitable. You should be grateful that a true Muslim is here to take this wealth."

The old man continued with his prayer beads.

"Yes, old man, it is time for you to pray. It is time for you to read your *Salat-al-Janazah*, your final prayer!" Abdali took one step back and then signalled his men. One of the Pathans held back the old man's head while another cut out his tongue. The old man screamed in pain, but no one dared to intervene as his blood dripped down his white *kameez* onto the floor. He collapsed in a heap to one side before the Pathans dragged him out by his feet.

"Clean this mess, and start the wedding preparations!" Abdali scolded his guards before returning to the throne. The guards began cleaning up the floor, and some court attendants were thrown to the ground and dragged over the floor until their own clothes were soaked in the old man's blood. The guards laughed and mocked the attendants. They cleaned the whole room and began the marriage preparations.

There was great pomp and celebration as the wedding ceremony was conducted quickly. Abdali retired to his quarters with the emperor's daughter and took a handful of maids with him as well. Others spent the night engrossed in lust and anger as the locals wailed out in pain.

The next day, Abdali decided his son Taimur was to be married too, so arrangements were swiftly made for him to marry a young woman. Another alcohol and *hookah* fuelled party was held in the palace. The emperor's attendants were forced to dance for Abdali and his lustful men. Great sin filled the palace and surrounding buildings as the party continued for days. While Abdali and his men were engrossed in lust and greed, the people of Delhi sat chained to the carts, barely fed and given any water. Some became ill due to starvation, while others were too weak to move or speak.

The old man had been paraded in the streets. No one had attended to him. He was tied to a post in the *bazaar* and left to die under the open sky. As the old man drew his final breaths, the prayer bead from his hands fell to the ground.

When Abdali decided to head home, all the carts were tied up. Abdali was seated on a large elephant with his new *begum*. He led the way as his men left the city. The loot was immediately behind him, followed by the captive women who wailed and cried aloud, but no one came to rescue them. The men and children made up the carts towards the back of the procession. The marriage party of sin left Delhi towards Kabul.

11.

Having accepted the *hukam* of the Dal Khalsa, the fearless Baba Deep Singh had mobilised a force of five hundred Sikh youth and left Damdama Sahib. All the Sikhs were on horseback. It was winter, and the night was very cold. Many of the Singhs were wrapped in black and blue woollen blankets. As they recited Gurbani, their swords glistened under the moonlight.

"Khalsa ji, you are to arrive in Thanesar overnight," that had been the *hukam* of the Jathedar. Every single Sikh was mentally preparing himself for battle.

Baba Deep Singh was riding on a white horse at the front. With him was his friend Sher Singh, whom he had known since arriving in Anandpur in 1700. They had been friends for fifty-five years and were known for their bravery, having fought many battles together for the Khalsa.

It was the middle of the night. There was a cold breeze in the air. The horses trotted at a steady speed, some nickering loudly and shaking their noses, others neighed in unison. The clip-clop sound of their hooves rang out across the jungle. The Singhs continued to recite Gurbani. The caravan of Singhs on horseback had another sixty miles to travel before they reached Thanesar.

"Jathedar ji," Sher Singh spoke before turning to Baba Deep Singh.

"These cold and wintery nights of Poh always remind me of those other nights of Poh …"

"Which nights," asked Baba Deep Singh.

"Those nights in which Guru Gobind Singh ji had to leave the forts of Anandpur Sahib. Those nights of the Khalsa travelling through Ropar and the Battle of Chamkaur. Those nights where Satguru's *Amaldari* was challenged by those worldly kings," replied Sher Singh.

"Sher Singh ji, you are very fortunate to have served the Guru during those times. I was not there for this *seva*," Baba Deep Singh said.

"*Hanji*, I think you returned to your village during that time, didn't you?"

"That's right. My parents had called me to return home for my marriage. However, I remember when news of the siege upon Anandpur Sahib reached my village that the Guru's four sons had been martyred, and many Sikhs were killed and lost. The Court poets and bards were forced to abandon Anandpur Sahib and Satguru's *Amaldari*, their governance, was directly attacked by the Hindu Hill Rajas and Mughal forces. I had to leave home immediately and had no time to wait for reinforcements. I remember jumping on my horse and riding as fast as the wind to reach the Guru. I only had faith in Akal Purakh, and crossing the Satluj River, I rode into Malwa."

Sher Singh listened as Baba Deep Singh recounted that fateful night and then interjected, "I remember how strong you were in those days. You had the strength of an elephant and the ferocity of a tiger. I'll never forget how you wrestled and killed Karam Din Pathan during the Battle of Chapparchiri. Even today, many of these young Singhs cannot compete with your level of strength and ferocity in battle."

Baba Deep Singh was very humble and deflected the praise:

"No, no, this is all possible because of Satguru's grace. The moment I claim to possess these qualities or the power to do anything is when I lose them. They are here due to the will of Akal Purakh, the one who creates, sustains, and destroys all."

Baba Deep Singh looked over at Sher Singh and continued, "I did not make it in time for the Battle of Chamkaur or the battles that followed, but when I reached the jungle in Malwa, I found a Sikh who informed me that the Guru had travelled to Sabo ki Talvandi with a few Sikhs after clashing with Mughal forces. The Singhs from Malwa had fought courageously and fended off the attack forcing the Mughal troops away."

Baba Deep Singh turned to check on the caravan of horses that were following. He then looked back towards Sher Singh and continued, "I had asked the Sikh how many Sikhs were with the Guru in Sabo ki Talvandi, and he had said about thirty or so, but he couldn't be sure of the exact number. That was all I needed to hear. I pulled Raki's reins, and we set off to have *darshan* of the Guru. We arrived shortly, and I went straight to the Guru's Darbar and bowed in reverence."

"Jathedar ji, you bowed at the feet of Satguru and liberated yourself. You are an inspiration to us all. The blessings Guru Sahib has placed upon your head are perhaps seldom placed on any other Sikh today." Sher Singh continued to praise Baba Deep Singh.

"Guru Sahib seemed very pleased. Embracing me, they said, 'We have been waiting for you to arrive. You are needed to complete a very important task here at Sabo ki Talvandi. We are just waiting on Bhai Mani Singh to join us.' I looked at Guru Sahib who then continued, 'you are going to do seva of the Granth.' Without thinking, I proclaimed, "*Sat Bachan*! I am unworthy, but as you wish. Due to the pull of worldly attachment, I returned home and left Anandpur Sahib. If I had stayed within your *hazoori* then perhaps I could have been of some service. Now I will never return home; I will stay here serving you and the Panth."

Listening to this, Guru Gobind Singh ji smiled. They loved the Singhs like their sons. Placing their hands on Baba Deep Singh's shoulders, they said, "Deep Singha! You have much seva to do for the Panth yet; there are difficult and dark times ahead, but you will endure them. You will also lead in the *parchar* of Gurbani."

Baba Sher Singh listened as Baba Deep Singh narrated the conversation from fifty years ago.

It was the middle of the night, and the stars were shining bright. The horses were walking steadily while the Singhs continued to recite Gurbani. Baba Deep Singh remembered various episodes from the past fifty-five years and continued narrating them to Baba Sher Singh. The Khalsa had endured so much to uphold the sanctity and sovereignty of the Guru's Darbar. They had shed their blood to fight the righteous battles and advance the Panth.

Baba Deep Singh continued, "We took up residence at Talvandi and took on the *seva* that Guru Sahib blessed us with – seeing to the horses, *langar* – how amazing were those days, Sher Singh! Absorbed in *seva,* no one tired, and no one was in pain or felt the need to be anywhere else. Things now are different; maybe it is because the body has aged, but those days within the Guru's Darbar were a true blessing that stayed with me and continues to empower me today." Baba Deep Singh continued:

"You are blessed, Jathedar ji, to have lived in such close proximity to the Guru. You are a true leader; your virtues inspire this generation and will continue to inspire the coming generations." Baba Sher Singh praised Baba Deep Singh.

"It is all Guru Sahib's doing. I have done nothing. All praise is the Gurus. We are just empty vessels drowning in the worldly ocean without the Guru," said Baba Deep Singh in humility.

Baba Deep Singh narrated the events from Sabo ki Talvandi where Bhai Mani Singh joined him. They were both entrusted with a great *seva*. After the siege and departure from Anandpur, many treasures of the Guru's Darbar were lost, including *granths* and *pothis;* some fell into the Sirsa river, while others were destroyed during the siege itself. The Guru asked for any remaining literature to be located and brought to them.

They then began compiling the Guru Granth Sahib; Bhai Mani Singh was the scribe, and Baba Deep Singh collected the paper, pens, and ink. Guru Tegh Bahadur's *bani* was added at this point. Both Gursikhs lovingly attuned their consciousness to the *Shabad*, and the immense *seva* was completed within the Guru's Darbar in nine months, nine days, and nine hours. The Sikhs also assisted in the bringing together of various writings that are today contained within Dasam Granth, the Granth of Guru Gobind Singh.

Upon completing this immense *seva,* Guru Gobind Singh began preparations to leave Damdama Sahib because they had decided to travel south and meet with Aurangzeb. Baba Deep Singh also readied themselves for this trip; however, Guru Gobind Singh stopped them and said:

"This place here at Damdama Sahib is now 'Guru Ki Kashi.' You and Bhai Mani Singh are to remain here and disseminate Gurmat far and wide. You are to teach others about Gurmat and spread *dharam*. If the need arises, you will also wage battle to protect and advance *dharam* in service of the Panth. Always remain ready for *dharamyudh*, the righteous war. When I leave this world, the Guruship will be passed to the Granth and the Panth. You must help ensure the Sikhs are taught about the Guru Granth and serve the Guru Panth. In the future, the Shabad will be the only support of the Gursikhs."

The caravan of horses continued to navigate their way through the darkness of the night. Baba Deep Singh recalled the Guru's *hukam, and* it rang out in his mind. Turning to Baba Sher Singh again:

"Baba Sher Singh, although the Guru is always *ang sang,* near at hand, these mortal eyes long for the vision of their *darshan*. Upon leaving for the south, they remained there, and I never had their *darshan* again. This is the reason my heart remains content at Damdama Sahib now. I never want to leave because those surroundings remind me of the Guru's walk and the Guru's talk. I am blessed with their presence in dreams sometimes, but when I open my eyes, there is just darkness."

"Jathedar ji, I will say it again, you are blessed. There are many in this world who call out for the Guru's *darshan*. To have been in their Darbar, listened and then acted upon the Guru's *hukam* is a big achievement, a huge contribution from which the Panth will only benefit."

"How so?" asked Baba Deep Singh.

"You compiled four copies of the Guru Granth Sahib and sent them to the four Takhts. For many months, day and night became one for you. I remember the days you would sit writing for hours with nothing but the flickering flame of the lamp to aid you. This *seva* will remain until the world stops spinning."

"Sher Singh ji, this is your misunderstanding … when you say that I did this or I did that, we do not have the capacity; whatever we do and achieve is through the power bestowed upon us by the Guru. Only when we face the Guru and become Gurmukh does the Guru grace us with the capacity to do. In many battles has the Guru made these arms move and advance the Panth forward."

"Jathedar ji, you are the embodiment of humility. Even in completing the *seva,* you do not allow yourself to slip and fall into the pit of ego. And this is why I say you are a complete *brahmgiani* – possessor of divine knowledge – as a Sikh who acknowledges the duality and dangers of lust, anger, greed, attachment, and pride; you are a role model to the rest of us."

Sher Singh was right. The *parupkari* Baba Deep Singh, at the age of seventy-three, was leading a Jatha of Singhs to stop the mighty troops of Ahmad Shah Abdali, before whom others, including the Marathas, Rajputs, and local Jats, halted and bowed. They had taken the easy route and accepted slavery.

At that moment, the evergreen Baba Deep Singh was full of youthful rigour, enthusiasm, and *chardikala*. They were armed with weapons, including their famous *khanda*, which had severed the bodies of many oppressors. Their physical strength and might were grounded upon the divine wisdom earned within the Guru's Darbar. They were the model of *sant-sipahi*, saintly-soldier, and had never refrained from waging the righteous battle. While Damdama Sahib was their base, they had completed many missions for the Khalsa.

When Banda Singh Bahadur accepted the Guru's *hukam* and travelled up to Panjab, Baba Deep Singh answered the call and assembled a Jatha of Singhs to meet Banda Singh. He had marched with Bhai Gurbaksh Singh, Sudh Singh, Prem Singh, Sher Singh, Dargaha Singh, Karam Singh, and others to join the Khalsa that had travelled with Banda Singh and reigned victorious over towns such as Sirhind and Sadhaura.

When Banda Singh established Khalsa Raj in 1710, Baba Deep Singh returned to Damdama Sahib and continued with the work of Gurmat *parchar* and dissemination. He oversaw the completion of the Granths that were sent to the Takhts and enlightened the Sikhs with Gurbani. Between 1715 and 1728, Baba Deep Singh spent his days writing Granths within the vicinity of lakhi jungle. Later following the *hukam* of Bhai Mani Singh and Mata Sundri ji, Baba Deep Singh travelled to Amritsar Sahib and took on the *seva* of head Granthi. Whenever the call came to serve the Panth, whether in the form of Gurmat *parchar* or to defend the weak and bring Khalsai justice to oppressors, Baba Deep Singh answered and delivered for the Panth.

Both Baba Deep Singh and Sher Singh continued to discuss the glory of Guru's Darbar and *seva* they were blessed to fulfil. Their conversation did not stop, but the journey soon came to an end. They reached Thanesar as the sun was resurfacing for a new day.

"We will stop here; let's tie the horses here and set up camp." Baba Deep Singh gave the order.

*****

"Bibi Rano ji, where was Baba Deep Singh during the formation of the Dal Khalsa?" Nihaal asked.

"He was largely based at Damdama Sahib engaged in Gurmat *parchar*, but whenever a call came from the Panth, as it did in 1755, Baba Deep Singh would immediately leave for where the Panth had directed him," explained Bibi Rano.

"Earlier you narrated that historic meeting of the Qaumi Jathedars in 1709, but can you tell us how the Panth grew again after Banda Singh Bahadur?" asked Jeet.

Bibi Rano nodded and continued with the story.

12.

In 1755, the Jathedar of the Dal Khalsa was Sardar Jassa Singh Ahluwalia. He was the one who had issued the news about Abdali's pending arrival and asked all major Sikh Misls to assemble along the main road connecting Karnal to the River Attock. They all had one thought in mind, to free the innocent prisoners who had been taken captive and take as much treasure and riches off Abdali as he passed through.

The treasure was to be reinvested into growing the Panth. The attacks on Abdali were never solely about personal gain or advancement. The Jathedar would see that each Misl was rewarded for their action, but the bulk of the money and treasure was retained for redistribution as the Panth deemed fit.

The first to arrive and answer the Jathedar's call was Baba Deep Singh, who had set up camp in Thanesar. When news of their arrival reached some local villagers, they prepared refreshments together. They soon arrived with barrels of *lassi* and simple food. Some of the Singhs cleaned and sharpened their swords, and others saw to the horses. In those days, the number of Singhs was not great, but they had become accustomed to guerrilla warfare. Striking in small bands and causing maximum damage before retreating, regrouping, and then going again. They were the tactics deployed by the Khalsa. Despite enduring the *choty a ghallughara*, the "smaller" genocide, the Sikhs remained steadfast in their duty to stand against oppression, defend the weak, and fight to advance *dharam*.

The responsibility to spread *dharam* rested upon the mandate to acquire political power and advance the Panth's sovereignty. The Sikhs understood that without political power and autonomy, it was impossible to spread *dharam*. To establish political power, the Sikhs were well aware of the necessity of bearing arms. There was no other agenda or objective in those days. While there were some Sikhs who took employment within the Mughal administration, such as Kauda Mal and Subeg Singh, they understood the importance of Sikh sovereignty and, on occasion, would assist the Khalsa.

The Khalsa operated under the authority established by Guru Nanak Sahib as Sache Patshah. They did not bow to any other worldly power. This was an integral part of the Panth created by Guru Nanak Sahib. Each Sikh was empowered to stand up and act upon the Patshahi bestowed upon them by the Guru.

The Vaisakhi of 1699 was not a ceremony of baptism; it was a declaration of war. A war against oppression, tyranny, corruption, and falsehood. This has been the way of the Khalsa since its inception.

*****

"Bibi Rano ji, where is the Khalsa today?" Nihaal interrupted the story.

"Well, son, some of the Khalsa are locked-up in jails across India, and some Khalsa continue to work towards re-establishing Sikh sovereignty. It is a very critical time now. Just like it was for the Sikhs in the 18th century after the two genocides. Many were killed, many were captured, and many more had to retreat to regroup. It is the same today, only now we have spread worldwide. The yearning for Sikh sovereignty is now felt by Sikhs across the globe."

Bibi Rano continued with the story.

*****

Many of the Singhs within the Jatha had fought bravely, and many had witnessed horrific scenes, but they remained in *chardikala* because their consciousness was attuned to the Shabad. They had full faith and love in Akal Purakh and were duty-bound to the Khalsa Panth.

After the capture and martyrdom of Banda Singh in 1716 along with hundreds of Sikhs, the Singhs were forced to retreat to the jungle to survive. Sitting in Damdama Sahib, Baba Deep Singh gradually grew the Jatha from ten to fifty to a hundred. Each battle brought new Shaheeds but also a new wave of initiates that joined the Khalsa. A time came when Zakhriya Khan became the Mughal regime's Governor of Panjab. At first, he appeared to want to work with the Khalsa, but he soon changed his ways. During those days, there was a price on the head of every Sikh, and many were captured and beheaded.

Zakhriya Khan was responsible for the torture and Shaheedi of Bhai Mani Singh and Bhai Taru Singh. He was eventually killed by the Singhs in 1745. After his death there was a split between his two sons. Yahiha Khan took over Lahore and gave control to Lakhpat Rai, a Hindu. He was full of *haumai* and only desired to increase his worldly wealth and power. He had a brother Jaspat Rai who was killed at the hands of the Singhs in battle. Upon hearing news of his brother's death, Lakhpat Rai vowed to avenge the death of his brother by launching a killing spree against the Sikhs.

Lakhpat Rai soon received the backing of Yahiha Khan and his forces. He found and burnt copies of Gurbani *pothis* and started to hunt Sikhs. He had told himself he could destroy the Sikhs and the Sikh Panth. He picked up many

Sikhs and killed them. Rivers of blood flowed through Panjab under his orders.

While many were killed in this way, the Khalsa remained steadfast and committed to the values of the Guru. They kept their *rehat*, and discipline, had full faith in Akal Purakh, and began training and preparing for what lay ahead. During this time, Baba Deep Singh led his *jatha* and joined the Dal Khalsa. The Singhs became stronger together, and their spirit grew. They would attack the imperial forces in large numbers and then retreat to the jungles. This tactic caused much damage to the enemy, who soon sent reinforcements.

The battles turned into a lengthy war, winter turned to spring, and spring turned to summer. Lakhpat Rai lost all sense of humanity and set fire to the jungles where the Singhs had set up camp. Baba Deep Singh took his *jatha* south towards the River Beas. They clashed with the halted their march, and the summer heat all worked against the Singhs, but they never gave in. They continued to march forward.

Baba Deep Singh was hit with injuries during those battles, but he remained steadfast. They eventually crossed the river. The terrain changed, but many of the Khalsa endured. The soles of their feet bled, they hadn't eaten or rested for days, but with Gurbani on their lips, they continued forth. It is a testament to the power of Gurbani and the pull of Gursikhi that those beloved Sikhs endured the blows of nature and the enemy but did not turn their backs on the Panth. Today many of us run away from Sikhi at the first opportunity, but those souls never gave up on the Guru. They soon arrived in Malwa.

They endured the autumn and winter months there, recouping and rebuilding. Soon enough, the month of Vaisakhi came around, and Singhs gathered in Amritsar. A major decision was taken with the passing of a Gurmatta, which declared that the time of retreating to the jungles had passed. Now the small *jatha* of Singhs needed to evolve into a larger *jatha* of Misls. Eleven different Misls were created with one objective in mind: Khalsa Raj. Baba Deep Singh became the head of 'Misl Shaheeda' and new initiates were recruited into the Misl.

In those days, two types of Singhs would join the Misls. The first were those who had full faith in Akal Purakh and were committed to the Sikh Panth. They would live as one large family. The other types were those who joined for the sake of fighting. Horses, weapons, and sundries became the priority. There was no desire for particular food or drink; whatever they received, they consumed. The Guru's *langar* was set up and shared equally by all.

Baba Deep Singh's Misl grew and became famous for its daring missions. The Singhs in this Misl were all imbued in *nam*, they were *kirtanis* and *likharis*. The Misl was known to include the bravest of brave *sant-sipahis*. The leaders of the other Misls all held Baba Deep Singh in high esteem. They all respected him as the overall leader of the Budha Dal. As someone who had lived and served the Panth within the *hazoori* of Guru Gobind Singh ji, Baba Deep Singh was honoured and respected by all. They always remained alert and ready to uphold the sanctity and sovereignty of the Guru Khalsa Panth.

This is how the decades between the Shaheedi of Banda Singh Bahadur and the establishment of the Dal Khalsa and Misls proved to be a defining period. The hardship of the times created resolute Sikhs who embodied the divine wisdom of Gurbani. That was their strength and support. The reason we remember and honour those Sikhs today is that they worked to deliver on the Guru's mandate. You will find photos of those warriors in Sikh homes and Gurdwaras worldwide. There are so many examples of defiance, resistance and *chardikala* that an entire library could be set up to house books on each of them.

If there is one commonality that binds them together, it is the continued pursuit of Sikh sovereignty. After the arrest, torture, and execution of Banda Singh Bahadur and the Khalsa with him, the Panth never forgot its purpose. They remained focused and aware of the political realities around them. Mata Sahib Deva, Mata Sundri ji, and Bhai Mani Singh led the Panth at a pivotal time, as did Jathedar Tara Singh Va, Jathedar Darbara Singh, and Nawab Kapur Singh in their own ways. In this way, Baba Deep Singh never abandoned the Panth for personal or familial gain.

The lure of serving another power, one far more resourceful than the Khalsa at the time, did not affect those dedicated souls who had pledged their mind, body, and soul to the Panth.

*****

Bibi Rano continued to narrate key moments from the 18th century as Nihaal and Jeet listened attentively.

13.

"The imperial army has arrived."

Baba Deep Singh listened as the messenger read the news.

"The imperial army led the march followed by Abdali, who sat upon an elephant. Behind him are more troops followed by thousands of carts of stolen goods and the women who have been taken captive. The entire procession is heavily guarded with Abdali's men flanking either side. Some have also ventured into the fields for a recon of the area. They plan to stop for the night soon."

The messenger was one of Baba Deep Singh's most trusted spies. He had become an expert in changing his guise to camouflage and blend in with the enemy. He had just arrived from Karnal with the information.

"What is the condition of those captured?" asked Baba Deep Singh.

"Very dire. Many of them are weeping; some have lost consciousness, while others appear lifeless, staring into an abyss. The women on the carts have little to no clothing, and the guards that walk and ride beside them are harassing them. They verbally and physically abuse the women who are calling out for someone to save them, but their cries are going unanswered."

Hearing this, Baba Deep Singh's blood began to boil. Turning around, he addressed the *jatha*, "Singho! It is time to display courage and bravery in this *dharamyudh*, but also high morals and ethics. You are to save those women who have been taken prisoner. They are this land's god-like mothers, sisters, and daughters; no one is to look at them with any lustful thought. Whatever money and treasure we retrieve from them will be distributed amongst you equally. Now let's get ourselves into five units of hundred Singhs. One unit will stay here in case the enemy attacks from behind. You are to fight them and push them towards Sirhind."

Baba Deep Singh explained the plan of attack to the remaining units. Many of the Singhs were battle-hardened warriors who had a thirst for *dharamyudh*; they thrived on the prospect of slaying the oppressor. They were fully committed to the cause and wanted to remove the invaders from their land and work towards the goal of establishing Khalsa Raj.

As they were preparing, another *jatha* of approximately two hundred Singhs arrived from Malwa. Most of the warriors in this *jatha* were young and eager for battle. They arrived with a resounding flurry of *jakaray*, the war cries of the Khalsa. Greeting the Singhs of Baba Deep Singh's *jatha* they sat and listened to where the attacks were going to take place. Whenever Abdali would come to loot and plunder Delhi, he would also raid the towns and cities on route. People had become used to this, so when news of his invasion reached them, they would run and hide in their homes. A lot of livestock and produce would be left unattended, cattle, chickens, sheep, lentils, beans, flour, butter, and sugar. All this was taken by Abdali and his forces too.

Baba Deep Singh jumped up onto his horse. Others followed suit. Most of the Singhs had two swords, a spear, a shield, and an assortment of smaller weapons on their person. They rode out together, but then each unit veered off towards its designated point of attack and began their wait.

The first jatha heard Abdali's procession of Singhs. His men were banging their drums loudly. They were in a festive mood, dancing and singing, thinking they had got away with all the loot and riches of the cities they had just raided. The Singhs from the first *jatha* allowed them to pass unnoticed. Then they saw Abdali sitting on top of his elephant. Next to him was *hazrat begum,* the one who he had forcefully married with little to no opposition from her father or any of his courtiers or guards.

Soon enough, the Singhs saw the carts, horses, camels, and donkeys, which carried the riches of loot. The women were seen as the spy had described. Some of them sat back to back since Abdali's men had tied them together by the hair. Others were tied at the hands and feet. His men walked beside them, carrying unsheathed swords and guns. They would often hit their captives with a stick or slap them as a show of power and control. They did not see the women nor the men they had taken prisoner as humans but as their newfound property. Most of these men and women were to be used and abused upon arrival in Afghanistan; others would be killed in public.

The women knew what was in store for them since they had heard stories of what had happened to others that were taken in previous invasions. They were praying and hoping for someone to save them and help keep their honour.

As they passed by the area where Baba Deep Singh's *jatha* was stationed, the Singhs heard their cries. Atop their horses, they crept forward in anticipation of the *hukam* to attack. Without turning, they readied themselves, one hand on the hilt of their sword and the other holding both ends of the reins. Some of the Singhs stood on the ground with swords in both hands.

"Akaal!" shouted Baba Deep Singh.

With that, the *jatha* leapt forward and pounced upon Abdali's forces with such ferocity and speed they did not know what hit them! Swords were swung with such accuracy and power that the wailing voices of the captives were quickly replaced with the cries of death from Abdali's men. Another wave of Singhs from the *jatha* attacked simultaneously, and the imperial forces had nowhere to run. Many were sliced open by the Singhs, who pounced upon them like hungry lions.

As Abdali's men began to fall, some Singhs turned their attention to freeing the captives. Women were released and taken to safety by the Singhs, who wrapped them in the blankets from their horses. The Singhs also then began to retrieve the bags of loot and riches. This first clash lasted about half an hour before that section of the procession retreated into the jungle.

Hundreds of Abdali's men were slain while a handful of Singhs attained *shaheedi*. The first attack was a success. Five carts of women were rescued and were sent back towards the camp.

With the tail end of Abdali's procession hit, the other units began their attack. As the procession passed the city of Ambala, they were met by units headed by Sardar Charat Singh, Jassa Singh Ramgharia, and others lying in wait. They caused much damage to Abdali's imperial forces. Hundreds of troops were killed with one strike as the Singhs reigned down one blow after another. They cut through the procession in no time. Many of Abdali's men ran away, dropping their weapons and allowing the Singhs to retrieve the loot and free the captives. By the time Abdali realised what had happened to the back end of his procession, it was too late for him or his men to put up any fight. Left with a few hundred troops, he decided to press forward and march on out of Panjab.

The released prisoners were brought to Damdama Sahib, where Baba Deep Singh personally saw to them all. He asked them where they were from, about their parents and where they wanted to go. Many were distraught and took time to speak up; others that spoke did not want to return home since they felt their parents would disown them. Many expressed a desire to stay with the Singhs at Damdama Sahib; however, Baba Deep Singh advised them against this. Like a loving father, Baba Deep Singh gave each one some money and items from the treasure retrieved from Abdali's loot.

After some time resting and recouping at Damdama Sahib, the women returned to their homes by a *jatha* of Singhs. Watching and hearing the Singhs speak and move, the women learnt of their high morals that shaped their character. They learnt about the Guru's Darbar and how the Khalsa was formed to root out oppression and create an egalitarian society where the welfare of all was looked after.

The women told others in their village about how the Singhs had rescued them and punished Abdali's men. Soon enough, their praises were sung from village to village. Those Singhs brought honour to the Khalsa Panth. Songs of their valour and courage became folklore, and

every home came to know about the revolution of Guru
Nanak Sahib.

14.

"Who were they? Where did they come from!?" bellowed Abdali.

"I don't just want them dead; I want to annihilate any sign of their existence. From here to Delhi, every single one of them will feel the brunt of my orders."

Abdali had set up camp in Lahore, where he was addressing his men. Pacing up and down, he was infuriated by the attack from the Singhs, which had caused him much damage and exposed the weakness of his troops. Turning to his son Taimur and general Jahan Khan, he said, "Tell me where they live; where should we strike?"

"O king, it is not easy to kill the Sikhs. They live in the jungles, the horses' saddles are their home, and they eat freely from whatever fruit the trees provide. It will be difficult to find them," replied Jahan Khan.

"I don't care where they live or how they survive! I want you to go and find them. They stole over half of the loot we took from Delhi and the neighbouring cities. They released those women and men who I had enslaved. So go, take as many troops as you need. Route them out and kill them all!"

"But my king, there may still be further danger ahead. We still have to cross the Ravi, Chenab, Jhelum, and Attock rivers. How do we not know more are lying in wait for us there?"

"If they are there, this time I will be prepared to crush their heads under the hooves of my horses. I have heard some of the *kafirs* are singing their praises, but when they hear about the manner of my victory over them, no one else will dare to sing of them let alone stand in my way."

Abdali continued to pace up and down his court. He addressed Taimur and Jahan Khan again, "You two must remain vigilant, don't get distracted with the singing and dancing here in the *divan*."

He paused and then looked out into the opening. "I have heard about the place they call "Chak Guru Amritsar. This is where they assemble, isn't that right?"

"Yes, my king. The troops have told me about this place. They say whoever so bathes in the waters in Amritsar they are liberated and attain salvation. The Sikhs visit all year, but especially so in the month of Vaisakhi," Jahan Khan explained.

"Very well," began Abdali. "Go there and destroy this place. Plunder and loot whatever is there and then turn the water red with the blood of the Sikhs! They will regret the day they thought about attacking me and taking my property!"

He continued to speak about the Sikhs and their places in a derogatory manner. After he finished his rant, Abdali sat back down. Turning to his son, he appointed him as the Subedar of Panjab and made Jahan Khan the head of the army. He left fifteen-thousand troops with them and set off with the rest towards Afghanistan. He crossed the Ravi river, but when he got to Chenab, Sardar Charat Singh attacked with the Singhs of the Sukerchakia Misl. They attacked with the same ferocity as before and killed many more of Abdali's men. As Abdali escaped, the Singhs retrieved more of the loot and freed more captives. After passing through the Khyber mountain range, he sent a note with a messenger back to Lahore. The note reiterated the order to attack and destroy Amritsar Sahib.

Jahan Khan was afraid of the Sikhs. The local maulvis had told him not to attack Amritsar because he would be committing a huge sin. They warned if he attacked and demolished the place Sikhs held sacred, a calamitous flood would ravage the land.

Taimur, on the other hand, wanted to act upon his father's order as soon as possible. He did not want to disobey because he had his eyes set on the throne.

Some months after Abdali had left Lahore, Taimur summoned Jahan Khan and asked him, "Why have you not dispatched the troops towards Amritsar yet?"

"*Sarkar*, I have sent spies to bring me information about their whereabouts. That being said, I have also dispatched a unit of troops under the command of the *haji* to search the jungle around Lahore and kill any Sikhs they encounter."

"Very well, but I want to ready the troops and leave for Guru's Chak immediately. You know the specific order my father gave."

Jahan Khan seemed to hesitate but then replied, "Yes, *sarkar,* I will prepare the troops today, and we'll leave first thing tomorrow …"

"No! I want you to prepare and leave today Jahan Khan!" bellowed Taimur.

Jahan Khan accepted and began readying the imperial troops. He went to his own residence, where his wife pleaded with him not to go. She prostrated with him not to attack since she had heard how sacred the Amritsar was. Many *sants* and *fakirs* arrived to hear Gurmat daily. Despite his own reservations, Jahan Khan was not one to disobey his king's orders. He pushed his wife out of the way and left in haste for Amritsar.

Upon arriving in Amritsar, Jahan Khan headed towards Harmandir Sahib. He ordered his troops to beat anyone who tried to stand in their way. Abdali had chosen Jahan Khan to lead his army because he knew he would stop at nothing. He had killed countless innocent men, women, and children at the behest of Abdali for years. He was known for publicly ridiculing his victims before killing them. As his men beat many innocents along the way to Harmandir Sahib, some of the women were picked up and thrown on the back of carts. Their children were snatched and separated from them as they were sent back to Lahore, where he planned to devour them later. Many of the traders were harassed and beaten, goods were stolen, and shops were smashed. Jahan Khan then turned in focus towards Darbar Sahib.

Unbeknown to Jahan Khan, at that time, Baba Gurbaksh Singh of Leelh had arrived to have *darshan* of Harmandir Sahib and do *seva* at the Akal Takht with a small *jatha* of thirty Singhs. They had set up camp in the Fort of Ram Rauni. The *jatha* of Singhs was full of *chardikala* and love for the Guru. They had pledged their mind, body, and wealth for the Guru's cause. News reached them of Jahan Khan's arrival. When they heard about his lowly actions, they all stood up and marched to Harmandir Sahib. They took part in an *ardas* and prepared themselves to defend the Guru's House. Baba Gurbaksh Singh addressed the Singhs:

"Singho! You have heard the news. The ego-fuelled fools think their attacks will go unanswered. You are standing upon the sacred land of the Guru's Darbar. Many before us have defended the sanctity and sovereignty of Darbar Sahib. We all know about Bhai Mani Singh, Bhai Mehtab, and Bhai Sukha Singh, who stood up to challenge these foolish ones. Keeping their actions in mind, you must remain steadfast and refrain from allowing the enemy in.

114

If the need arises, we will all stand and fight until our final breath today and fulfil the Guru's bachan … "*sava lakh se ek larrao.*"

All the Singhs responded with a resounding *jakara* as they accepted the challenge of just one taking on thousands! Baba Gurbaksh Singh spoke again:

"Today, we stand like the Guru did with the Khalsa in Chamkaur Sahib. The enemy will surround us with thousands of troops and launch its attack, but we will hold our positions."

The Singhs were joined by a handful of local Sikhs who had full faith in the Guru and were prepared to stand with the Khalsa to defend Darbar Sahib. They waited until they could hear Jahan Khan's troops outside the *parikarma.* He had sent some troops to Fort Ram Rauni, but most of his force was with him. As he ordered his men to enter the *parikarma* of Darbar Sahib, his men faced a barrage of arrows fired from the Akal Takht, where Baba Gurbaksh Singh had stationed the Khalsa.

"*Bole so nihal! Sat Sri Akaal!*"

"*Akaal hi akaal!*"

"*Satguru teri ott!*"

The sound of war cries from the Khalsa followed the volley of arrows. In those days, the land immediately behind the Akal Takht was not built upon, and on that day, it turned into a battlefield as the Khalsa waged war to defend the invaders. Jahan Khan had never witnessed such ferocity in battle. He had never experienced the speed with which he saw his troops fall that day. Any moment his men tried to advance towards the *parikarma*, they were struck down with arrows. Soon enough, the Singhs were engaged in close combat. Spears and swords swung as heads rolled and bodies dropped to the ground.

The ground soon turned red, and heaps of bodies began to pile up. Baba Gurbaksh Singh was in the centre, leading the charge as he swung two swords with speed and power. The imperial troops landed hits, but they were not fatal. As the battle raged, some Singhs began to fall and attained *shaheedi* behind the Akal Takht.

Jahan Khan sent reinforcements, and soon enough, just four Singhs remained. Baba Gurbaksh Singh let out such a *jakara* that it was as though a bolt of lightning had scorched the ground – Jahan Khan's troops were sliced through their armour as many began to run from the battlefield. He watched from afar and then signalled further reinforcements to enter. The Singhs began to take hits but continued to fight with the same intensity. After taking numerous hits, they fell to their knees but swung their arms across the ground to sweep up and kill the enemy. Baba Gurbaksh Singh and the final Singhs eventually fell. Their bodies were riddled with cuts and blows as they delivered on their *ardas* and attained *shaheedi*. Today Gurdwara Shaheed Ganj stands behind the Akal Takht on the ground where this battle took place.

The Singhs all attained *shaheedi* as they defended Darbar Sahib. Jahan Khan signalled his troops to head towards the *parikarma,* and they stopped in between the Akal Takht and Harmandir Sahib. Turning to his troops, he gave the order, "Now it is time to put down your swords and spears …" He paused, then smiled and continued, "You don't need them anymore. Now it is time to pick up the guns and the cannons! Demolish this entire place!"

His men obeyed, began demolishing the small houses on the *parikarma,* and threw the rubble into the water. They made their way to Harmandir Sahib and did the same there. Orders to loot and plunder the surrounding buildings and shops were also given.

As Jahan Khan watched, it is said he heard a voice emanate from where Darshani Deori stood, "O fool, this pool, and these buildings will remain forever, and the city of Amritsar will stand long after you have gone." Upon hearing this voice, Jahan Khan looked around but did not see anyone. He thought it was his mind playing tricks; after all, he thought, *my religion allows me to attack and destroy the place of kafirs.* He recalled the stories he had been told about how his forefathers had looted and plundered before him. Their actions empowered him to do the same and gave him a sense of authority.

The city of Amritsar felt the force of Jahan Khan's order; however, it is said some of his men sustained many injuries while demolishing Harmandir Sahib. As a result, Jahan

Khan brought in commoners who lived in the surrounding vicinity. They refused but were beaten and forced to commit the atrocity of tearing down the Guru's abode.

By the next day, Jahan Khan's men had razed Darbar Sahib to the ground. He set up camp and told his men to ensure no one lit a lamp. Any sign of life was to be exterminated. Upon giving this order, he headed towards the Beas river in the direction of Kartarpur Sahib, where he plundered more places of Sikh importance.

The deputy Jahan Khan had left in Amritsar began his watch. He ordered some men to demolish more houses and threw the rubble into the *sarovar*. No Sikh was found to be seen. All the Hindus and Muslims remained indoors, too afraid to come out in case Jahan Khan's men put them to work.

As the sun set, a small flame appeared to flicker on one side of the *sarovar*. The deputy was shocked because he had not seen anyone enter or leave. As he approached the light with some of the men, he saw that it was indeed a *diva* which someone had lit recently as the oil was full to the brim and the wick was still long. The deputy kicked it and threw it into the water.

The next day, the deputy sat with a few men near the *Dukh Bhanjani* tree. The sun disappeared, and Amritsar was engulfed in darkness. As he scanned the ground, to his bewilderment, another light flickered on the opposite side of the *sarovar*. He jumped up and ran over with the men to try and grab the person who had lit the lamp. They searched and searched but found no one. The deputy then turned around to notice the lamp had disappeared. There was no sign of it. As they huddled together, the lamp reappeared on the adjacent side and seemed to glow even brighter.

"Sarkar! Something is not right. Jahan Khan has made a mistake by ordering the demolition of this place. There are forces at work beyond our comprehension," one of the men addressed the deputy.

Walking away, the man mumbled, "Jahan Khan has signed his own death warrant. We need to get out of here."

15.

One candle can light many candles. A small fire can quickly become a large fire if more fuel is added. In this way, one scholar can inspire many scholars, which can create a movement of knowledge production and dissemination. Baba Deep Singh was a *sant-sipahi* and well-respected scholar, having spent many years learning in Anandpur Sahib and then spreading the wisdom of Gurmat all over Panjab. He had taught many other great scholars and inspired many Sikhs towards the path of Sikhi.

Since the time spent with Bhai Mani Singh in the *hazoori* of Guru Gobind Singh, writing and explaining the depths of *ilahi bani*, divine wisdom, Baba Deep Singh had written many *pothis,* and his *likhai,* calligraphy, was quite exceptional. It was truly beautiful. He had taught and guided so many onto the path of Sikhi, and in doing so opened a school for budding Sikh scholars.

In 1757, Baba Deep Singh turned 75. He had served in the Khalsa Panth for 57 years, ever since he had travelled to Anandpur Sahib with Mata Jeoni and Bhai Bhagtu to take Amrit from the hands of Guru Gobind Singh. His old age was not a deterrent to any physical ability. He was as strong and agile as many of the youthful Singhs in their prime. He could ride a horse with the same speed and wield this double-edged sword with equal power and swiftness. As a scholar of Gurmat, he was a *brahmgiani*, and as a warrior, he was commanding on the battlefield. He had a powerful aura, radiating love and compassion to all.

One day in the late autumn months of 1757, Baba Deep Singh was sat speaking to his nephew, Sada Singh.

"*Gumukha!* We have received news that Abdali has declared war on the Khalsa Panth. I may need to leave for Lahore soon."

Hearing this Sada Singh replied, "Baba ji! If you are going, then I would like to accompany you. I, too, have a yearning to fight for *dharam*."

Even though Baba Deep Singh was Sada Singh's uncle, he addressed him with the honorific title of Baba.

"No, son. You do not need to go," replied Baba Deep Singh.

"Why?" asked Sada Singh.

"I have educated and trained you as a scholar. Your duty is to remain here and spread the wisdom of Gurmat. Teach *santhia,* the correct pronunciation of Gurbani, and explain the *arth,* meaning, of what Guru reveals to us in the Shabad. There is no greater work than teaching and spreading Gurmat."

He smiled and then paused before continuing, "This is your *seva,* Sada Singh, and you must fulfil your duty no matter what happens."

"I am still young, Baba ji. I need more time to fully teach and inspire others like you do," said Sada Singh.

Turning towards the open fields, Baba Deep Singh spoke again, "The Guru will bless you. Have *sharda,* full faith, and love in the Guru, and all your work will be completed. What are we without the grace of the Guru? None of us have any strength of our own; whatever capability and capacities we have are all due to the blessings of the Guru. What little strength and wisdom I have comes from the grace of the Guru."

Sada Singh continued to listen.

"As long as you keep your *rehat,* read your *nitnem,* serve the *sangat,* and do an *ardas* before the Guru, you will have all the power you need to accomplish your task."

Baba Deep Singh looked back towards Sada Singh. "I have this feeling that we are going to have to endure some really testing times, but with the Guru's support, just as we have endured the decades following their departure and the *shaheedi* of Baba Banda Singh, the Khalsa Panth will forever remain in *chardikala* until it reaches its goal."

Baba Deep Singh was absorbed in deep contemplation and continued to offer words of wisdom to Sada Singh, who was keen to learn more about the goals of the Panth.

"*Dharam,* righteousness," Baba Deep Singh spoke.

"*Dharam* is the goal of the Panth. It is a very clear instruction from the Guru. To spread *dharam*. This is why Guru Nanak Sahib founded Kartarpur Sahib. It was a space to nurture the Gurmukhs through Sangat and Nam, and when the Guru in their 10th form felt the Sikhs were ready, they revealed the Khalsa. The role of the Khalsa is to protect and further the Panth's interests."

"How does the Panth strive to establish *dharam*?"

"*Raj bina na dharam chale hai, dharam bina sab dale male hai* – without *dharam*, the whole world wanders around aimlessly. So *dharam* is a must, but *dharam* cannot be established without first establishing your rule. This is the way of the Khalsa and why Raj is so important for the Khalsa. Raj begins with the Guru – *nanak raj chalaia, sach kot satanee neev de* – in Gurbani we read how Guru Nanak established Raj, built on the foundations of truth."

"So, until the Khalsa establishes raj, we cannot fully spread *dharam*?" asked Sada Singh.

"Right, but that *raj*, that rule must be based on *halemi raj* – a model of governance based on Gurmat, based on *sarbat da bhala, sanjhivalta, parupkar* – that is a type of governance based on the welfare of all life forms, one which promotes a shared co-existence and governance that is truly benevolent. These values are not just abstract ideas that the Guru speaks about Sada Singh, but they were physically manifested by the Guru with the founding of the Guru's Darbar, from Kartarpur Sahib to Anandpur Sahib. We take

123

inspiration from what the Gurus achieved, but the *parchar* of Sikhi must always continue. Whether Sikhs have Raj or are struggling to establish their sovereignty, we must continue to spread Gurmat, preserve our *maryada,* and inspire the next generation. For this reason alone, it is important for you to remain here and continue with this task."

They sat and spoke for a while as Sada Singh continued to ask Baba Deep Singh about the role of the Khalsa in uplifting society and creating a better world.

Soon enough, the conversation shifted back to Abdali, "As I said, we have some testing times ahead of us. We must stay vigilant and in *tyari*. We still haven't received any news of how Abdali took the attack on his *kafla*, although we know he was chased away by our brothers from the Sukarchakia and Bhangi Misls," said Baba Deep Singh.

We still haven't received any news.

Just as Baba Deep Singh spoke those words, a Singh arrived and greeted them. He was drenched in sweat and looked very tired as if he had been travelling for days.

"Vaheguru ji ka Khalsa Vaheguru ji ki Fateh!"

Baba Deep Singh and Sada Singh greeted the Singh respectfully and sat him down next to them.

"Baba ji, I have come from Tarn Taran!"

"Dhan bhag!" you are blessed, came the reply.

The Singh looked up with a worried expression.

"What is the matter, Singh ji? Did you hear anything on route?"

"They have committed a great sin! Abdali, his son, his subedar, the deputy – all of them!" said the Singh.

The messenger's name was Bagh Singh, and he was a young Nihang who was engaged in *seva* at Tarn Taran Sahib when he heard about what had happened.

Baba Deep Singh stood up and looked directly into Bhag Singh's eyes. He asked, "What have they done?"

"They have demolished Ram Ghar … Harmandir Sahib and the Akal Takht have been reduced to rubble," came the reply.

"And what about Baba Gurbaksh Singh?" asked Baba Deep Singh.

"Baba ji and the Singhs in their *jatha* all attained s*haheedi* after putting up a strong defence. They punished many of Jahan Khan's men but ultimately left their bodies performing the highest *seva*." Bagh Singh explained how they all fought valiantly until the last breath.

He stood with Sada Singh as both witnessed Baba Deep Singh close his eyes, his fists clenched and chest out. With his head tilted upwards, Baba Deep Singh stood motionless for what seemed an eternity. It was as if he had gone into *samadhi*, a deep state of meditation. Then without warning, he opened his eyes and let out a resounding *jakara*, which Bagh Singh and Sada Singh both acknowledged with proclamations of *"Akaal, Akaal!"*

"I have been bestowed with the *hukam*. May Satguru be my support." Baba Deep Singh spoke in an assured voice, palms clasped together. Bagh Singh and Sada Singh remained standing and listened as Baba Deep Singh spoke again:

"When the home of the Guru is attacked, a Sikh cannot continue with worldly affairs. The tyrants have committed such an act, now is the time for nothing but a swift and precise response. A world without the Guru is a dark place for the Sikhs. Now is the time for action."

"Bhai Sada Singh!"

"*Hanji*"

"You are to continue with the upkeep of this place. It is your responsibility to ensure the *santhia* continues as normal. Serve the *sangat langar* and ensure the *parchar* of Sikhi continues. I am going to ready the Singhs and leave for Amritsar immediately. The Khalsa will celebrate the coming *divali* there after delivering on the *hukam* of Guru Sahib."

Baba Deep Singh instructed Sada Singh to beat the *nagara,* the war drum, and ready the horses. Within minutes, the whole of Damdama Sahib was on its feet as news of the desecration in Amritsar reached them. The horses were readied and loaded with an assortment of weapons. The *nagara* continued to resound as Baba Deep Singh, the benevolent, the complete *sant-sipahi* sat cross-legged with eyes closed and hands resting on his knees, palms down. This moment was immortalised as the iconic image that every Sikh holds so dear. Baba Deep Singh sat in s*amadhi* with the name of Har on his lips and war on his mind.

16.

"Singho! The foolish ones engulfed in worldly attachments and desires have committed an atrocity that only deserves one answer. The time for battle and *shaheedi* is upon us. Come out wearing your new clothes; we are going to marry death. Bring your best weapons and join us in Damdama Sahib."

This was the *hukamnama* that Baba Deep Singh sent with Bhai Sada Singh, Baba Naudh Singh, and Dyal Singh, who delivered it to the villages across Lakhi Jungle. They had taken small *nagaras* on horseback. Every village they stopped in heard the war drum and the message from Baba Deep Singh.

"Following an order from the Subedar of Lahore, Taimur Shah, son of Ahmed Shah Abdali, the ego-driven Wazir Jahan Khan has desecrated Guru ka Chak. The *sarovar* at Amrtisar has been defiled with the rubble of surrounding buildings. The Akal Takht and Harmandir Sahib have been demolished. This is a direct attack on the Guru Khalsa Panth, which requires an immediate response. Whosoever wishes to drink the nectar of martyrdom, join us in Damdama Sahib, where preparations are being made to leave with a large *jatha*."

This order was read out to all residents, Sikh and non-Sikh. Those who held love and respect for the Guru began to gather their weapons and horses. Many of the new people that arrived had little to no training in warfare but were willing to support those who did in any capacity. Some were too distraught with the news of the attack, while others cried out in anger:

"Jahan Khan will meet the same fate as Massa Rangar. Does he think there are no more Sukha Singhs and Mehtab Singhs left?"

"There are many things Singh can endure, such as iron bars and torture, but such an act will never go unpunished."

"It's time for *shaheedi – dharam sir ditia baaj nahi rehana, dharam sir ditia baaj nahi rehana!*" Righteousness cannot flourish without giving one's head in the time of need.

Listening to such outcries, many stopped what they were doing and joined those preparing to leave for Damdama Sahib. They got changed into new white clothes, tied a new *dastaar*, and picked up their finest weapons; an assortment of swords, spears, shields, and daggers. Many young sons turned to their mothers and bid them farewell. One Singh called out:

"Ma! Wish me well. I am going to fulfil the ultimate *seva* for the Guru. I am going to complete the journey that began in your womb. Bless me Mother; bless me with your hands. Baba Deep Singh awaits my arrival. I am going with the Singhs to deliver on the word of the Khalsa."

The brave mother lovingly embraced her son and bowed to his *dastar*. She broke her worldly attachment to create an undying bond with the Guru and the Khalsa. She guided him to his horse and handed him his sword. Elsewhere a sister saw off her brother,

"Go veer, but return victorious!"

Another sister called out:

"Take as long as it takes brother. I'll see to the fields. May the Khalsa always remain in *chardikala*, and may the Guru's Khalsa never refrain from righteous action. May we perish, but the House of the Guru stay forever strong."

Some of the Singhs that had mounted their horses shouted back with resounding *jakaray*. One young Singh looked towards his wife and said, "I am going; may the Guru be your support. Make sure you tell our son his father attained *shaheedi* in *dharamyudh,* martyrdom in the righteous battle! Give my sword to him and raise him in *tyari,* to be ever-ready in service of the Khalsa Panth."

In this way, many Singhs mobilised to leave their villages and join Baba Deep Singh at Damdama Sahib. Someone left their mother, someone their father, someone their siblings, and others their wives and children. They all left their worldly attachments to forge the true connection that would liberate them and their entire linage.

Others found it harder to part with their loved ones, but the Singhs had full faith in the Guru. A new bride who still had *mehndi* on her hands and a *choora* around her wrists pleaded with her husband to stay and keep her youth intact. She clasped her *mehndi* full hands, and tears rolled down her eyes. But the beloved of the Guru smiled and gave his wife encouragement:

"Bhai Joga Singh did not get to complete the fourth *laav,* the Guru's *hukam* needed to be answered. If you listen, you'll hear the Shaheeds calling too. Sri Darbar Sahib has been desecrated, and the Akal Takht has been destroyed, and you want me to sit at home? I cannot do this. If I stay at home and die laying on the couch from a snake bite, then what will you do? At least this way, my love, I can still remain victorious with the Khalsa."

"You do not know what will happen in battle," she said.

"Very well, may Guru be my support."

The Singh called a *fateh* and left with the others.

Amongst the *chardikala* Singhs there was a group of youth who had heard about the daring accomplishments of Baba Deep Singh and the Khalsa. They all had a deep sense of love and loyalty, but because they were not Khalsa themselves, there was a sense of apprehension from them. They did not believe themselves to be worthy of fighting in *dharamyudh*, of defending the sanctity and sovereignty of Darbar Sahib.

Sensing their hesitation, Sada Singh wandered over and asked them, "So then, what will it be? Are you prepared to join us in Damdama Sahib?"

The eldest of the youth was called Pal. He looked up at Sada Singh and spoke, "We are not ready Bhai ji; we are not worthy of such service; look at us – we still cut our kes. We are a long way off what Baba Deep Singh demands of us."

Pal lowered his head and wrapped his arms around his knees, which he had pulled up close to his chest.

Another young boy called Jassa spoke.

"Bhai ji, we've heard the stories about Banda Singh Bahadur, Nawab Kapur Singh, and Baba Deep Singh – we are working towards becoming like them, but look at us; we are a million miles from them."

Sada Singh smiled and addressed them.

"My brothers, this is the beauty of Guru Nanak's House; you only need to walk towards the Guru and strive to become Gurmukhs; the Guru will do the rest. You take one step towards the Guru, and the Guru will take a thousand steps towards you. Have some faith in yourselves. Have some self-belief that you are worthy of walking on this path of Sikhi. You'll have the support of the Guru and the sangat of such *chardikala* Gursikhs around you. What else are you waiting for?"

The youths looked at each other.

"But we have nothing, Bhai ji. We come from low caste families and–" before Pal could continue, Sada Singh interjected, "Nonsense! There are no divisions of caste in the House of Guru Nanak. Tell me what you need, weapons? Horses? There is no shortage of supplies here. I will get you what you need; you just have to ask."

The youths looked at each other. Pal stood up and looked at the Sikhs who were hurriedly gathering supplies, loading their horses, and readying their weapons. He looked at the mothers who were blessing their sons and turned back to his friends and spoke, "This is our time brothers. We have to make the effort like Bhai ji has said. I have full faith in the Guru, even though I may not be worthy. What better cause is there to fight for than the cause of the Guru? The Gurmukhs will make us worthy!"

"*Shabash*, brother! That's the spirit!" Sada Singh put his hands on Pal's shoulders and embraced him.

Jassa stood up, too, followed by the others. Each gathered what little they had with them and followed Sada Singh. He took them over to a *jatha* of Singhs that were readying their supplies. Feeling empowered, the youths joined in, merged with the *jatha*. Sada Singh came back with a *gutka sahib* and a handful of different *shastars*.

"These will be your friends from now on. Keep them safe, clean, and maintain them daily. Always keep the *gutka sahib* close by and read *gurbani* daily." He spoke these words and then disappeared into the crowd to help others.

The group of friends adorned one *shastar* each and handed the pouch, which contained the *gutka sahib* to Pal. One of the Singhs from the *jatha* came over and secured the pouch to Pal's waist with a blue *kamarkasa.* He looked at Pal and said,

"Look at that. It's as if you've always been a part of our *jatha.*"

The friends travelled with the *jatha* of Singhs through Lakhi Jungle and arrived at Damdama Sahib, where thousands had gathered. Some were there to leave for battle; others had come to see them off.

Baba Deep Singh stood in the middle, unwavering and immovable like a mountain in the middle of a storm. His electric blue *bana* glistened in the reflection of his fifteen-kilogram *khanda* that he raised to the sky. Lowering it, he drew a line along the ground between him and those who had arrived.

"Singho! Those of you who have arrived in readiness for *dharamyudh,* in readiness for *shaheedi,* it is now time. If you wish to join me as I march to Amritsar, then step over this line with the Guru's Bani on your tongue – *pehla maran kabool, jeevan ki shad aas"* – the Singhs replied with – *"hohu sabna ki rehnka, to aou hamare paas"*- first accept death, give up worldly desire, become as humble as the dust under your feet and then join me. Guru Arjan Sahib's words reverberated around Damdama Sahib as thousands of Singhs crossed the line.

"Do not fear the enemy, even if they are more resourceful. Today we will defend the sovereignty and sanctity of Sri Darbar Sahib with our *khanday* and *talwars.* This will always be the case. Even when the enemy canons of today transform into seemingly impenetrable metal vehicles of the future, even then a beloved of the Guru will always defend Sri Darbar Sahib, even if he has but one *teer* in his hand."

Every Singh was armed and dressed in new clothes, ready to marry death. The *nagara* was struck, and the *narsingha* was blown. The war drums and war horns echoed as the caravan of battle-ready Singhs left Damdama Sahib. With Gurbani on their tongues and war on their mind, the *jatha* soon reached the blessed grounds of Tarn Taran Sahib. They all bathed in the sacred sarovar of *shaheeda de sirtaj* Guru Arjan Sahib and awaited further orders from Baba Deep Singh.

17.

Afghan kings and emperors always looked forward to the evenings. After their *namaz*, they would indulge in all manner of lustful activity and consumes intoxicants. These evening *divans* were known as *mehfils.* They would hold these after looting and plundering towns and cities. At the *mehfils,* they would consume alcohol, smoke tobacco, and bring in dancing girls for their pleasure.

Following his fourth invasion, Ahmed Shah Abdali had left his son Taimur in Panjab as the Subedar. The *wazir* was Jahan Khan. They both relished the time spent in *mehfils.* Although Taimur had recently married in Delhi, and Jahan Khan had two wives, both men also kept a concubine of young slave girls. In those days, the existence of concubines in which women were enslaved and exploited was common practice amongst all three Abrahamic religions. Thousands of women were taken by Abdali back to Afghanistan and kept in *harems.*

Taimur had set up his encampment within the Lahore Fort built by Shah Jahan. One evening shortly after the desecration of Darbar Sahib, he was sitting in the *mehfil* surrounded by his dancing girls. The room was covered in red and green velvet drapes, and bottles of alcohol lay scattered across the room. Some of the women were passed out while others were being forced to continue their dance. Standing beside Taimur was a twenty-two-year-old Iranian dancer called Jhamile. Her cat-like eyes had cast a spell over him. A jewel encrusted necklace draped down her chest, and she swayed from left to right pouring liquor into his mouth. In front of him were four other dancing girls who were easy prey to his lustful gaze. Taimur felt invincible and was revelling in the environment that surrounded him. His eyes moved between each dancer, scanning them from head to toe. Totally engrossed in the moment, his senses were mesmerised by the sound of their anklets as their feet tapped the marble floor.

Jahan Khan entered the room as Taimur's mehfil was in full swing. He too had indulged in his own mehfil, but a messenger from the city of Patti had shaken him out of his intoxication. Jahan Khan moved swiftly through the room until he reached Taimur.

"Oi …" slurred Taimur, "get your own girls; these are mine." Grinning, he pulled Jhamile down, and she stroked her hands down his bare chest.

"Sarkar, the messenger from Patti, has arrived with some alarming news," Jahan Khan said.

Taimur was not within his senses, and the words did not register. He tilted his head back as Jhamile instinctively poured more liquor into his open mouth.

"Sarkar, thousands of Sikhs have assembled and are marching on us. The messenger says they have crossed the Beas River."

Taimur's eyes opened. He pushed Jhamile's hands off him and wiped his mouth.

"What!?" he proclaimed. "You told me they had been killed and that you had demolished their Amritsar."

"I did, sarkar," replied Jahan Khan.

"So where have thousands more sprouted from?" Taimur raised his voice as he tried to fight off the drunkenness.

Sensing a change in the air, Jhamile stopped her dance and reached for her clothes. The other girls followed suit and began to get dressed. The musicians stopped, and the whole atmosphere changed.

Enraged, Taimur shouted, "Oi, why have you *kanjaria* stopped? Start the music again; I'm not finished here!"

Jahan Khan tried to speak, "But sarkar …"

"But nothing. We are sat here inside the Fort of Lahore, heavily guarded, and they live in the jungles with nothing to their names. Take a unit and deal with them once and for all, Jahan Khan!"

Turning to the dancers with half glazed eyes, he shouted, "You dance and sing until I tell you to stop!"

The dancing girls looked towards the musicians, who looked towards Jahan Khan. There was a moment's silence before it was broken by a thundering voice.

"NO! Wake up, boy! This is no joking matter. They are marching in thousands. We need to ready all the troops!"

Jahan Khan had never addressed Taimur in this way, but his outburst pulled Taimur out of his slumber, and he regained his senses. Although Taimur was the Subedar of Panjab, Jahan Khan was twenty years older and had served Abdali all his life. Taimur realised this was a serious matter, and Jahan Khan was right.

"The issue may escalate quickly if we do not act now. They could even mount an attack on Lahore," Jahan Khan continued.

Taimur rubbed his eyes and tried to get up. The rush of blood to his head was too much, and he stumbled back. Jhamile tried to help, but he pushed her away. Looking back at Jahan Khan, he said, "What should we do? It is dark outside too …"

"In matters pertaining to rule, there is no difference between day and night. And these Sikhs, they do not differentiate between day and night … once they make up their minds they can forsake food, drink, and sleep. They must have plans to reach a particular location overnight. Their Guru has not taught them the ways of comfort, but the ways of endurance and resistance."

Taimur continued to listen and shake off the drunkenness as Jahan Khan spoke, "Our army is spread out at the moment; we have about five thousand with us here at Lahore."

"Ready those troops and order Haji Atai Khan to set off and stop the Sikhs in their tracks. They should leave overnight. Send a message to the deputy in Patti too. Do it now!" Taimur ordered.

"Very well, *sarkar*. You should get ready too."

Taimur slowly got up from his chair and walked back to his quarters. Jahan Khan spent the night in a state of apprehension. His *begums* were also awake as they saw him question aloud how the Sikhs could be on their way in such large numbers.

"Thousands are marching towards us. It is clear they are coming for blood. It feels like a *toofan* is coming. Who will stop them?"

Listening to him question himself aloud, his younger *begum* spoke, "Do not go with the troops to face the Sikhs."

"Why not?"

"I have heard they are fearless and have the support of their Guru. No one has been able to stop them. The previous Mughal emperors of Delhi couldn't stop them, even when they martyred their leaders. They are steadfast and will seek revenge."

"They are fearless? No one is fearless. I demolished their Harmandir Sahib, and no one could stop me."

"That is because they were not there at the time. Those handful that did try to stop all embraced death, but your army suffered huge losses. I have heard it all, and I am sure they will seek full revenge. Please, do not go with the troops."

"I am the *wazir* and head of the army in Panjab. The Sikhs are closing in, and if I do not go, do you think the Badshah will forgive me? He will ask for my head the moment he receives news of it. We will fight the Sikhs and beat them … I am not just relying on our troops …"

"So who else are you relying on … *khuda?*"

"In the name of *khuda,* I will mobilise my men to launch a *jihad.* In the name of Islam, I will raise the *Haidri* flag and recruit thousands of young men into the army. The Sikhs are probably no more than ten to twenty thousand in number. The one leading them in this march is an old man, a scribe from what I gather. What does he know about warfare and fighting on the battlefield? No warrior has been born from the land of Panjab to beat your Jahan Khan. You'll see."

Jahan Khan may have said those words to his *begum,* but inside, he was scared. He did not sleep much that night. He kept waking up after a few minutes, managing no more than two hours of broken sleep.

The next morning, all the drummers were gathered together. Each one was handed a green flag and were given the following order:

"By the grace of Ahmed Shah Abdali, the Subedar Taimur Shah has given an order to which all the Qazis and Mullahs support, that the Sikhs are nearing the Fort of Lahore, and they wish to uproot the Islamic regime. All youthful and able-bodied men should come to the Fort and join forces with the army. Bring your weapons and come on horseback. The army will march out this afternoon; we are to head towards the Guru Chak in Amritsar!"

Hearing this, some locals joined the army while others, who knew of the Sikhs and their fighting prowess, hid in their homes. Others ran away.

Jahan Khan led the army out of the Fort of Lahore that afternoon. His men mustered a distance of around six *koh* before they set up camp near Sarai Khana. The next morning, they set off again and eventually stopped two *koh* from Darbar Sahib.

The arrival of Jahan Khan and his men alarmed the locals. Many of them closed their shops and went home. They could sense the men arrived with violent intent, and the locals were not prepared, nor did they want any part in it.

Jahan Khan ventured forward towards Darbar Sahib and set up his camp there. One of his spies came with information. "The *shaheedi jatha* of Sikhs is on its way. They are marching and singing songs of martyrdom. They do not fear death. Ten thousand of them are coming!"

"Where is Haji Atai Khan?" asked Jahan Khan.

"He is not here. The Nawab of Patti is on his way through ..." said the spy.

"Go and find Haji Atai Khan. He was ordered to meet us here with his men," Jahan Khan interrupted.

"Sarkar, he is Adina Beg's man, and as you know, he had his own intention to become the Subedar of Panjab ..."

"I see," said Jahan Khan as he paused and stroked his little beard. "So he hasn't arrived because he wants to see us defeated at the hands of the *kafirs* because then he will have a chance to become the Subedar."

"Maybe they are working together."

"Where are they now?" asked Jahan Khan.

"They have assembled at Tarn Taran and are organising to march here. They have a large number of weapons and are making full battle preparations. More continue to arrive from Majha, Malwa, and Doaba. They speak of their *dharamyudh.* The battle will commence in two days."

Jahan Khan was listening to the intel from his spy when one of his lieutenants arrived.

"Sarkar, Karim Khan is here …"

"What does he want?"

"He is saying it is urgent. A female spy has been captured."

"Who is she?"

"She is a Sikh woman, sarkar."

"Bring them both inside."

The lieutenant walked out of the tent. A few second later, the six-foot seven-inch frame of Pathan Karim Khan entered. He greeted Jahan Khan and then spoke, "We have found a woman. She appears innocent, but I think she is putting on an act. She is very clever. She says she is a Sikh; she must be a spy."

"Where is she?"

"Come with me. We have captured her because she is a threat."

"One woman is a threat to the imperial army of Ahmad Shah?"

"Yes, *janab*. You will see."

Karim Khan led Jahan Khan out of the tent. They walked some distance away from Darbar Sahib towards an open field area where a woman was tied to a tree. Her long black hair was draped out over her shoulders and partially covered her face. Her *salwar* was torn, and her *chuni* had been used to tie her against the tree. Despite her predicament, she gazed back at the two men with sharp hawk-like eyes. As they neared, she clenched her fists.

"Let me go! ... Tell me, where is Jahan Khan?"

Jahan Khan walked closer and asked her who she was.

"I am the mother of a *shaheed*, wife of a *shaheed* – Singhni – my name is Daleyr Kaur from Sultanvind.

"Why are you here?"

"To kill Jahan Khan … where is he?"

144

The woman did not flinch. She continued to speak without fear.

"One woman here to kill me?" Jahan Khan spoke out and started laughing. *She must be insane,* he thought.

"You … you're Jahan Khan?!" the women began to laugh loudly. Staring at Jahan Khan, she continued to laugh and then spoke, "You are such a coward. You're scared of one woman, yet speak of fighting against the Singhs? How will you fight against the lions of Guru Gobind Singh? You thought you killed my husband and son, Sham Singh and Ram Singh, as they defended Harmandir Sahib, but they did not die; they became *shaheeds.* They have become immortals here at Darbar Sahib, where a lamp still flickers, and a light will always exist here, Jahan Khan, but you … you will die. Tell your soldiers to let me loose, and you'll see how I am your death. I am a Singhni. I am a daughter of Guru Gobind Singh ji, and you're about to regret ever being born!"

"So you are a spy?" Jahan Khan tried to divert the conversation.

"A spy for who?" he asked.

"The Sikhs who are marching here?"

"They do not need a spy. They are walking here, having already pledged their life in service of the Guru. They have no care for their personal safety. They have no attachment to this world. I am here to seek revenge for my husband and my son. I heard you would be here, so I left my home,

145

but your men took my sword off me. They are so cowardly and fearful of one woman. You have no idea what the Singhs will do when they get here. They will hit your entire army like a storm, and the whole world will remember this battle for generations to come."

Listening to the fearless words of Daleyr Kaur, Jahan Khan was hit with worry and doubt. He ordered her to be killed. "She is dangerous and a threat, kill her."

"Kill me. What else can you do? I have come to attain *shaheedi*, what other job do I have?"

Upon hearing the order to kill her, Daleyr Kaur remained in *chardikala* and began to laugh.

The Pathans untied Daleyr Kaur from the tree and then retied her hands with rope. An executioner was summoned from within the ranks. He looked at her, and Daleyr Kaur laughed in his face.

"Come on! Raise your sword and kill me then! This is the justice your rule delivers. Jahan Khan should be the one being executed here, he has the blood of thousands on his hands, but you want to kill me because I speak the truth, You want to strike a blow on an unarmed captive woman." Daleyr Kaur continued to taunt her executioner.

"Kill her, now! What are you waiting for?" Jahan Khan shouted in anger. He was completely overcome with fear as Daleyr Kaur's eyes pierced through to his soul.

"Kill me but hear one more thing before you do," began Daleyr Kaur. "Your rule will not last. It will be over within two years, and you will not be found anywhere. I am the messenger of death for your entire regime."

Daleyr Kaur had no fear of anyone. Her words continued to shake Jahan Khan to his core, and even the executioner's sword began to tremble. She was steadfast in her Sikh principles and values until the very last moment.

"Kill her!" came the deafening sound of Jahan Khan's order.

As the executioner tightened his grip on the sword's hilt, Daleyr Kaur taunted him, "Do it. I don't want to live under such oppression. I want to attain *shaheedi* and only ask that I be reborn into the House of the Guru time and time again to challenge oppressors like you."

At that moment, the executioner swung down and struck Daleyr Kaur, who laughed her way to *shaheedi.*

Jahan Khan stepped back and stood alone. For the first time in his life, he felt his entire body overcome with fear.

18.

The Singhs bathed in the sarovar at Tarn Taran Sahib. *Guru ka langar* was prepared, and they all ate. The horses were also fed and provided with water. Others had joined Baba Deep Singh's *jatha*, a large assortment of weapons was being cleaned and readied for battle.

Baba Deep Singh stood for an *ardas* in which he asked for Satguru's blessings as the Sikhs were ready to embrace death to uphold the sanctity and sovereignty of the Guru's House. Following the *ardas*, Baba Deep Singh jumped onto his horse and led the rest of the *jatha* out. With him was Baba Naudh Singh, Dyal Singh, Gurbaksh Singh, and other brave warriors. They were fearless and ready for *dharamyudh*. All the Singhs had immense love for the Guru and the Panth. They left Tarn Taran Sahib for Darbar Sahib, adorned head to toe in different weapons.

As they neared, news reached Baba Deep Singh that Jahan Khan had set up his troops near Chabba and was awaiting their arrival. The Afghan forces were great in number and had a larger firepower in their overall artillery and arsenal.

"Very well, we will commence our charge from here. Horses will lead the way with the rest of the *jatha* walking on foot," said Baba Deep Singh. Turning to the rest of the *jatha,* he continued, "This *dharamyudh* will inspire the Panth, who so ever attains *shaheedi* here will find a place at the feet of Guru Sahib. This *seva* is the highest *seva* for the Panth, and every one of you who marches with me today will receive the blessings of the Guru because of the *ardas*."

Then Baba Deep Singh spoke his final words to the *jatha*, "Singho! Keep on moving forward. Do not run from the battlefield. We must reach Darbar Sahib. Do not try and avoid the enemy that stands in our way; face him head-on. We are here to attain *shaheedi* and restore the sanctity and sovereignty of the Guru's House, which has been attacked and taken over by these ego-fuelled invaders. Remain firm, stay in *chardikala,* and remember the Guru's words – *sir deeje kaan n keeje* – let us now show these Haidri flag bearers why the Guru created the Khalsa. Let's show the world the power of the Khalsa!"

Saying this, Baba Deep Singh tapped his horse with his heel. The horse neighed loudly, stretched his legs back as though he too was doing a *namaskar* towards the direction of Darbar Sahib, and then leapt forward. He galloped at full speed as if the desire of *dharamyudh* had awoken with him too. Immediately behind Baba Deep Singh was Baba

149

Naudh Singh and Baba Dyal Singh, both of whom could be seen riding at full speed towards Darbar Sahib. There was a whirlwind of dust, and then behind them came a *jatha* of approximately three thousand Singhs. The ground shook, and the sky trembled with the sound of *jakaray* as the Khalsa gathered speed.

They neared the town of Chabba. As per the plan, some of the Singhs cut across the fields to remerge from the left, others from the right, and another *jatha* went straight through the middle of the town, while two others overlapped the side flanks to enter from the other side. Jahan Khan's men were waiting in the centre and were completely unprepared for the strategic attack. Many Afghan troops were overcome with fear at the sight of the full bearded Singhs with their razor-sharp swords, spears, and arrows. The deafening sound of *jakaray* and the speed of their movement was overwhelming for many who ran before any blows were struck.

Within Jahan Khan's entourage was a Lahore-based reporter called Miskeen, who was charged with recording the whole battle. He was trained in *farsi* and was an enthusiastic writer. Miskeen wrote:

"The Sikhs had caught wind of our arrival in Chabba, and they encircled us from all sides. They launched their attack like a pack of wild lions; each one smiled and laughed as he sliced our men with one blow. Many of our troops who witnessed this from the inner circle began to run, but there was nowhere to go. The Sikhs were possessed and were muttering words before loudly proclaiming, *"Akaal hi Akaal!"*

Baba Deep Singh had a large sword in his hand. He was swinging it on the battlefield with such precision and speed that it was difficult to tell which head fell from which torso. The screams of anguish from the Afghan troops were only drowned out by the *jakaray* that continued to reverberate across the town of Chabba.

Screams of *"Ya-Ali!"* were followed by roars of *"Akaal Akaal"*

The sound of steel on steel accompanied the battle cries as the Khalsa unleashed a wave of fatal blows. The Afghan and Pathan fighters, who outnumbered the Singhs, managed to strike back, delivering some fatal blows of their own. The ground was soaked with the blood of fallen warriors. Horses were seen running off into the wilderness as the men they once carried lay in pieces across the ground.

Kasam Khan from Patti was well-renowned for his speed and agility on the battlefield. Having heard stories about the Singhs but never seen them fight with his own eyes, he too, had arrived in Chabba to witness the battle. In addition to his men, his *begum* and servants were also with him. He sat atop his red horse and initially watched from afar. After seeing the carnage unleashed by the Singhs, he kicked his horse towards the battlefield. With shield in one hand and sword in the other, he leapt off his horse and began fighting on the ground. Jassa Singh from Malwa saw him enter and immediately headed towards him. Raising his swords in the air, Jassa Singh shouted:

"Let's see what you're really made of, Kasam Khan; let's see if you're ready to clash with the Singhs of Guru Gobind Singh!"

Kasam Khan responded with some taunts of his own as he changed his footwork and began to encircle Jassa Singh. In one swift movement, he went to strike Jassa Singh, who was able to duck. Kasam Khan came again from the other side, but Jassa Singh blocked the strike with the sword in his left arm. Seeing an opening, Jassa Singh swung the sword in his right hand and took Kasam Khan's head right off in one gracious move. His body collapsed in a heap, and the head rolled towards the battlefield, where it was trampled under the hooves of Varyam Singh's blue horse. Seeing this, Kasam Khan's *begum* and servants screamed and ran from the battlefield.

The Singhs continued to pile up Afghan and Pathan bodies in pitched battles across the town. The enemy saw how much damage each of the Singhs was doing, so they brought in reinforcements. An assortment of guns was distributed, and cannons were assembled.

A little further up from where Jassa Singh had decapitated Kasam Khan, Baba Naudh Singh was waging battle. He was a true servant of the Guru's House and a ferocious warrior whose sword hit the enemy like a bolt of lightning. Jahan Khan encircled Baba Naudh Singh with a dozen men, who like a pack of hyenas, began to attack from all sides. Baba Naudh Singh was able to defend himself like a lion, but the hyenas managed to deliver some blows to the body of Baba Naudh Singh. Despite the cuts and wounds that had opened up, the Khalsa continued to fight. His blue *chola* had turned a crimson red, and blood trickled down his white beard. His trustworthy horse took many blows and ultimately fell to the ground after the enemy fired shots. Baba Naudh Singh managed to stand up despite the bullet wounds. Jahan Khan's men encircled him again on their horses, firing bullets from the front and back. Baba Naudh Singh took the blows but never ran from the battlefield.

Seeing this, some of the men pulled their horses back. They had never witnessed a man take so many hits and continue to stand. It was not human. They did not know what inspired and empowered Baba Naudh Singh to stand and continue to laugh in the face of death. They did not know he meditated on Akal, kept a strict Khalsai discipline, and wanted to embrace *shaheedi* defending the sanctity and sovereignty of Darbar Sahib. They were worldly men doing a job they were paid to do. Baba Naudh Singh was a *dharmic*, spiritual man voluntarily doing the work of the Guru.

Those that remained there continued to strike Baba Naudh Singh, who fell to his knees but kept his *khanda* tightly gripped. He was unable to move his arms to raise his weapons, but his eyes continued to pierce the enemy's soul as he attained *shaheedi*.

The *shaheedi* of Baba Naudh Singh enraged the Singhs even more, who raised their voices and bellowed *jakaray*. The war cries echoed from the other side of the battlefield. When the blood of such spiritual men drenched the ground of Chabba, it raised the battle standards of the Khalsa even more.

While the battle had now stretched across the town, Baba Deep Singh continued to lead the charge from the front. He was like a man on fire; no one was able to stop him. Anyone who tried to stand in his way met their death. Many of Jahan Khan's men had stopped trying to engage with Baba Deep Singh. They also told others in the army to stay back as they believed he had superpowers.

Jahan Khan was enraged and began to berate his men, "Go! Move forward and fight him! We have to stop him; we have strict orders to kill them all here before they reach Guru Chak."

None of his men dared to engage with Baba Deep Singh, who continued to move towards Darbar Sahib. In a fit of rage, Jahan Khan began to attack his men for their disobedience. Like a man possessed, he swung his sword, causing mayhem in their ranks.

"If you do not obey the Shah's order, you will be killed anyway!" he continued to shout. "They have lost great numbers, and they have no reinforcements. I have dispatched a messenger to Taimur Shah. He is sending a fresh unit. Victory is in sight. Have some belief in *khuda* and stop these *kafirs!*"

The men saw no victory, just death in the form of the Khalsa that was relentless on the battlefield. They had never encountered such a fighting force and were losing all hope.

No sooner had Jahan Khan spoke, Haji Atai Khan arrived with a large battalion of men and horses. The reinforcements took their toll on the Singhs, who had been fighting all day.

Haji Atai Khan was a well-renowned general of his time. He was a fearless warrior on the battlefield, but he stood from afar to watch as Baba Deep Singh sliced through the enemy with ease.

Time appeared to slow down as the skies opened for the demigods to take their seats for the spectacle that was about to unfold. On the ground, Baba Deep Singh picked up speed, unleashing fatal blow after fatal blow upon the enemy. As a whirlwind of dust from the battle surrounded them, the sound of steel hitting steel reverberated across the battlefield. Baba Deep Singh's double-edged sword was ushering in a new world, in accordance with the *hukam* of Akal Purakh, but he was struck on the neck by an enemy soldier. At that point, it is said Baba Deep Singh's head fell from his body.

Seeing this, one of the Singhs shouted to the others, "keep on fighting!"

He moved towards Baba Deep Singh's head to move it so that the enemy could not step on it. As he went to lift the head, without thinking, he said:

"Baba ji, you had said you would not rest your head until we reached the *parikarma* of Sri Darbar Sahib. The boon of *shaheedi* is awaiting us there, and a Singh never wavers from his words."

At that moment, Baba ji's body straightened up and stood back on its feet. The *khanda* was still clenched within the right hand. Without any assistance from the Singh, Baba Deep Singh's head found its place on his left palm. Witnessing this, all those who were fighting nearby stopped in their tracks. For a moment, both sides forgot they were in a battle. Many began to rub their eyes and shake their heads in bewilderment as Baba Deep Singh's body moved forward, *khanda* in one hand and head in the palm of his left hand.

The *khanda* moved with the speed and power of the propellers of a helicopter. It was difficult to see the *khanda*; there was just a rapid flash of circular light, which glistened around Baba Deep Singh.

"Hai Allah! What is this!" many of the Pathans started to shout.

"How is the decapitated body of the Sikh walking and continuing to fight?!"

As Baba Deep Singh continued to advance towards Sri Darbar Sahib, many of the Pathans went into a state of shock. Some dropped their weapons, and others simply froze, not knowing whether their eyes had mistaken them. Others who saw Baba Deep Singh coming stepped back, opening a way for the advancing warrior who continued to swing his *khanda* slicing enemy soldiers.

On the other side, as Singhs witnessed the *kirpa* of Satguru, which had empowered Baba Deep Singh to fight with his head in the palm of his hand, they became even more resolute.

"Akaal hi akaal!" shouted the Singhs
"Khushia de jaikarai gajave nihaal ho jaave sat sri akaal!"

The war cries of the immortals resounded across Chabba. A new wave of strength ran through the Khalsa. Those who had suffered several cuts and blows looked down at their injured limbs and laughed. Their injuries now seemed inconsequential in the presence of their Jathedar who fought with his head on the palm of his hand. The imperial forces from Afghan began to feel the power of the Khalsa as many were slayed. The road through Chabba towards Darbar Sahib became a graveyard for the Afghan fighters. It was as if a new river was being forged in Panjab; only this one flowed with the enemy's blood as their bodies made up the embankment. Death danced

157

everywhere but the immortal frames of the Khalsa. The demigods watched as Baba Deep Singh marched towards the abode of Sodhi Sultan Guru Ram Das Patshah.

The final stretch saw countless Afghans meet their end as Baba Deep Singh, chief of the Shaheeda Misl, and the Singhs fought ferociously. Many of the enemy forces had fled from the battlefield. As they neared Darbar Sahib, the Afghans positioned cannons and began to fire towards the Khalsa. The great warrior Dyal Singh who had fought so bravely attained *Shaheedi*. Just like Baba Deep Singh's otherworldly actions had inspired the Singhs, the fall of Dyal Singh brought a new wave of encouragement to keep the *dharamyudh* going.

The skies turned grey, and large clouds formed above. Baba Deep Singh manouvered between the cannon fire.

"Oh Satguru, please help me reach your sanctuary; may I not stop until I reach the *parikarma*. If I am to be blessed with *shaheedi,* then that too must be attained at your feet," Baba Deep Singh called on the Guru for support.

It is against Gurmat for one to display miracles for self-pleasure or gain, or indeed for the entertainment of others. But here, Baba Deep Singh was empowered by the Guru to uphold his Ardas and the sacred vow taken to punish those who desecrated Sri Darbar Sahib.

It was 11th November, 1757, the day of Diwali. A time when Sikhs from far and wide would travel to bathe in the sacred *sarovar* of Sri Darbar Sahib. It was also the anniversary of the day Bhai Mani Singh had attained Shaheedi because of the refusal to pay tax that had previously been rendered void between the Khalsa and Mughal Governor in Panjab. It was almost fate that on that day, the Khalsa was once again engaged in battle.

Despite being a renowned warrior of his time, Haji Atai Khan had not entered the battlefield until the first wave of Singhs had attained *shaheedi*. He had heard about the Singhs but witnessing them first-hand had instilled a sense of fear within him. He knew others were looking towards him, so to save face, he had reluctantly entered the battlefield just before Baba Deep Singh placed his head on his palm. Haji Atal Rai's seven-foot frame trembled uncontrollably with fear. He had mumbled some words to himself, "*hai khuda …* this is a sign from you."

He had lost all intent of advancing as the Singhs were stepping foot onto the ground, which immediately preceded the sacred *parikarma* of Sri Darbar Sahib.

Turning to Jamal Din, he scolded him, "Go on ahead and stop those *kaffirs* from entering their Guru's place! If they enter, we will lose all respect. Jahan Khan is either dead or will die from his injuries. Look at how many of our troops have been slayed. There is just a handful of Singhs left, go … go and stop them from entering!"

"Sarkar, how can we stop them? They are fighting with their heads in the palm of their hands. It feels as though whomever we cut down, he gets back up and continues to fight. They just don't lie down, even after meeting death!" Jamal Din responded with a look of utter disbelief.

Angered with this response, Haji Atai Khan shouted, "I don't care! Whatever happens, we must stop them from entering! Your job is to accept my orders!"

Jamal Din lost all his senses and rushed forward towards where Baba Deep Singh was fighting.

"I don't know if you are a Sikh or some other unknown being, but I, Jamal Din, have come to stop you," he spoke, raising his sword in the air.

At that moment, the heavens opened with deafening sounds of thunder. Baba Deep Singh's eyes glanced towards Jamal Din; not saying any words, he smiled, and battle commenced. Baba Deep Singh struck Jamal Din, who retreated and stuck out his shield in a desperate attempt to stop the blows, which struck like lightning bolts.

"Ya Allah" shouted Jamal Din. He responded with some of his own powerful strikes. One … two … three … four swift blows, but each one met the khanda of Baba Deep Singh. He had no shield because his shield hand was balancing his head. After the fourth strike went empty, Baba Deep Singh spun his khanda back around, bringing it crashing across Jamal Din's neck with an almighty strike. His head rolled off to the right as his motionless body collapsed in a heap to the left. Jamal Din's head continued to roll until it was crushed under the hooves of oncoming horses.

As the heads of the Afghan soldiers rolled, the remaining forces now began to retreat in large numbers. Shrieks of anguish, pain, and horror were heard all around. The Singhs, however, remained determined to advance.

As the Singhs entered the Sri Darbar Sahib, Baba Deep Singh launched his head across the *parikarma*. It flew over the fighters before landing near the *sarovar*. In this way, Baba Deep Singh upheld his *ardas* with the support of Satguru. He attained *Shaheedi* while defending the sanctity and sovereignty of the Guru's Darbar.

Where his body fell, Gurdwara Shaheed Ganj Baba Deep Singh stands. Where his head finally rested in the sanctuary of the Guru, another memorial stands. A timeless reminder of the Divine power infused within the Khalsa of Guru Gobind Singh ji Maharaj.

19.

Nihaal and Jeet sat quietly as Bibi Rano completed the awe-inspiring account from Sikh tradition. She paused, closed her eyes, took in a deep breath, and exhaled, *"vaheguru sache patshah."*

The children joined in as she recited *mool mantar*. A little time passed before Bibi Rano led the children through some *simran*. They sat for a while in this way, cross-legged on the floor of the *langar* hall.

Nihaal looked up at the paintings hung around the *langar* hall and spotted the famous portrayals of Baba Deep Singh. The paintings had always appealed to him, but now that he knew the events which led to the artwork around him, he felt a deeper sense of belonging and gratitude. He looked at the painting, which depicted Baba Deep Singh drawing a line in the ground with his Khanda, which had marked the beginning of that defence of Sri Darbar Sahib.

He scanned the other paintings of Sikh warriors from the same century and then moved onto the Sikhs from the 19th century. As Bibi Rano completed the *Simran,* Nihaal's gaze stopped on another image. This one was a little different from the others. It wasn't a painting but a photograph.

Nihaal looked at the Sikh in the photo; he wore a dark blue *dastaar* and had a long black flowing beard. In his hand, he held a *teer*, a spear. Nihaal was drawn in by the Sikh, and he remained fixated on the photo.

Bibi Rano noticed Nihaal looking, and she said softly, "Do you know who that is Nihaal?"

Nihaal had seen the photo before but couldn't quite remember the name.

Jeet looked up and instantly knew who it was.

"That's Sant ji!" she exclaimed.

Bibi Rano smiled. "*hanji puth*, that's right, it is Sant Jarnail Singh ji Khalsa Bhindrawale, the 14th Jathedar of the Damdami Taksal – the same Taksal of Baba Deep Singh."

Nihaal looked up.

"He, too, led a defence of Darbar Sahib, but we don't need to go back centuries to learn about their *seva*. It only took place a few decades ago, in 1984," said Bibi Rano.

"Abdali's men attacked Darbar Sahib again?" asked Nihaal.

"No, no, son. This attack was not from Abdali or his men. The attack on the Sikhs in 1984 was ordered by Indira Gandhi and the Indian government, who sent army tanks and demolished Darbar Sahib."

"Why?" asked Nihaal

"Similar reasons to Abdali, but the response from the Sikhs, led by Sant Jarnail Singh was inspired by the actions of the 18th-century shaheeds that I've just told you about.

The response in 1984 from Sant Jarnail Singh and the Khalsa was so powerful that it awoke the entire Sikh Panth around the world," Bibi Rano explained.

Nihaal stood up and walked over to the photo. Bibi Rano and Jeet followed him.

Placing her hands on his shoulders, Bibi Rano spoke, "We'll save that story for another day."

Glossary of Terms

Akal Purakh – The Timeless Being

AL-Lat - Arabian goddess of war and combat, known in Greek mythology as Athena.

Amrit – Nectar of Immortality, as prepared by Guru Gobind Singh in 1699

Amrit Vela – Ambrosial hours of dawn

Ang Sang – Forever near

Antim Ardas – Final supplication

Ardas – Supplication

Baba – Grandfather, also used out of respect to address an elder man

Bhatts – Ballad singers

Bir Asan – Warrior's pose

Bir Asan Bani – Warrior's mantra, also used to refer to Guru Gobind Singh ji's *Dasam Granth* (writings).

Budha Dal – Senior Army, employed mainly for garrison duties requiring less mobility

Bunga – Military barrack

Chandi – sword, also used as reference to Hindu goddess of war

Chardikala – Sikh doctrine of an ever-rising spirit

Chola – Traditional warrior dress

Chuni - Headscarf

Dal Khalsa – Army of the Khalsa

Dasam Granth – Guru Gobind Singh ji's writings

Dastaar – Turban

Degh – lit. Kettle used to refer to food prepared in communal kitchen

Dharam – Righteousness, also used as synonym for faith

Dharamsala – lit. A place to learn about the practice of a religion, also place of meditation

Dharamyudh – the righteous war/battle

Dharmic – To be of a righteous nature

Dharmraj – One who judges our actions after death

Divan Khana – Political office

Dumalla – Turban worn by Khalsa warriors

Fateh – Victory, also a salutation for the Khalsa, as in Vaheguru ji ka Khalsa, Vaheguru ji ki Fateh

Firanghi – Foreigner, a term used for the British

Gatka – Sikh martial art

Granthi – An individual learned in *Gurbani*

Gurbani – Guru's Word

Gurdwara – lit. Doorway to the Guru, also used as name for Guru's House

Gurmatta – Political decision-making assembly of Sikhs

Gurmukh – One who obeys the Guru

Gurmukhi – Guru's script

Haveli – House

Jatha – Unit of Sikhs

Jathedar – Head of unit of Sikhs

Ji – Used as a show of respect, normally after addressing someone by name

Jujharoo – Sikh fighter

Kabaddi – Panjabi sport

Kalgi – Royal plume

Kalgidhar Pita – Guru Gobind Singh ji, the wearing of the plume

Kamarkasa – Cloth tied around waist

Kavishris – Poets

Khalsa – Collective of initiated Sikhs

Khalsa Raj – Sikh rule

Kirpan – Sacred sword

Koh – unit of distance. 1 koh is approximately 1.8 miles

Kurta – Panjabi dress

Langar – Food from Guru's communal kitchen

Mahal – Royal palace

Mala – Rosary beads

Mandir – Hindu place of worship

Manja – Wooden bed

Manmukh – One who obeys their own mind, does not listen to the Guru's Word

Maya – Illusion or Duality

Mela – Festival

Misl – Military unit, also term used for territories acquired by the Sikhs

Nagara/Nagaray – Battle drum(s)

Narsingha – Battle horn

Nawabs – Officers of land

Nishan Sahib – Sikh flag

Nitnem – Daily recitals for Sikhs

Panj Pyar-e – Five beloved Sikhs of the Guru

Parikarma – Pathway surrounding Harmandir Sahib in *Amrit*sar

Patshah – Sovereign

Pentra – Style of battle movement

Phulkari – Panjabi design

Pita ji – Father

Ranjit Nagara – War drum

Rehat – Discipline

Rehras Sahib – Daily prayer for Sikhs normally reciting around sunset

Sadhana – Daily spiritual discipline

Sadhus – Saints

Salvar – Dress

Sant-Sipahi – Saint-Soldier

Sarbat Da Bhalla – Welfare for all, a key Sikh philosophy

Sarkar – Your highness/your majesty

Sarovar – Reservoir/tank of water

Satguru's Amaldari – The Guru's governance/Raj

Sati – The act of a widow jumping into her husband's funeral pyre

Shabad – Guru's Word

Shahzade – Prince

Shastar Vidhia – Science of weaponry

Shiv ji – Hindu god

Sikh Sardars – Sikh Chief

Simran – Meditation
Sindoor – Small line of red powder above the forehead, a sign of a wedded women

Singhni(a) – Daughter(s) of Guru Gobind Singh

Sochi – Panjabi sport

Sohila Sahib – Daily prayer for Sikhs normally reciting at night, before going to sleep

Taruna Dal – Junior Army

Tegh – Sword

Tyar-bar-tyar – Ever ready

Ustad – master/teacher

SHAHEED AKALI BABA DEEP SINGH